Self Heal.
One Day It Just Clicks

Who You Are is up to you. Give yourself 1 hour and you will look at the world from a different angle

Minii Begum

Copyright © 2021 by Minii Begum.

All rights reserved. This book is protected by copyright. No part of this book may be reproduced or transmitted in any form or by any means, including as photocopies or scanned-in or other electronic copies, or utilized by any information storage and retrieval system without written permission from the copyright owner.

Under no circumstances will any blame or legal responsibility be held against the publisher, or author, for any damages, reparation, or monetary loss due to the information contained within this book, either directly or indirectly.

Legal Notice:
This book is copyright protected. It is only for personal use. You cannot amend, distribute, sell, use, quote or paraphrase any part, or the content within this book, without the consent of the author or publisher.

Disclaimer Notice:
Please note the information contained within this document is for educational and entertainment purposes only. All effort has been executed to present accurate, up to date, reliable, complete information. No warranties of any kind are declared or implied. Readers acknowledge that the author is not engaged in the rendering of legal, financial, medical or professional advice. The content within this book has been derived from various sources. Please consult a licensed professional before attempting any techniques outlined in this book.

By reading this document, the reader agrees that under no circumstances is the author responsible for any losses, direct or indirect, that are incurred as a result of the use of the information contained within this document, including, but not limited to, errors, omissions, or inaccuracies.

Printed in the United States of America.

Interior Design by FormattedBooks.com

Table of Contents

Introduction vii

Chapter 1: Core Beliefs—We Are Our Choices 1
    Our Personal Core Beliefs 2
    Negative Core Beliefs: The Childhood Connection ... 6
    Current Core Beliefs Become Habits 8
    The Good vs The Bad 11
    Shifting Your Negative Thought Patterns 14

Chapter 2: Deep Breaths, Less Stress—Be Mindful 19
    The Art of Living Mindfully 22
    Mindfulness Matters 27
    Being Mindful at Work 31

Chapter 3: Self-Awareness—Be Aware of the Present 35
    Can You Be Too Self-Aware? 39
    The Three Levels of Self-Awareness 42
    The Significance of Being Self-Aware 46
    Social Awareness with Others 49

Chapter 4: No. It is a Complete Sentence—
    Stretch Your Boundaries 54
    Boundaries Can Be Difficult to Set 56

Boundaries Can Be Fragile 60
Handling People Who Cross Your Boundaries 63
Healthy Family Boundaries 66
Healthy Relationship Boundaries 67
Healthy Professional Boundaries 70

Chapter 5: One Moment. One Decision. One Action—
    Start Today 72
    You Can Alter Your Life 73
    Career Changes 76
    Pushing Through the Difficulties 79
    Proactive vs Reactive Behaviour 82
    Beating Procrastination 84

Chapter 6: Accepting the Bad with the Good 88
    What is a Good Life? 89
    Deciphering Destructive Behaviours 92
    It Is Okay to be Sad 95
    Acceptance 97
    Instant Gratification 100

Chapter 7: Raise Your Words, Not Your Voice. Be an
    Adult 103
    Avoiding Immaturity: Acknowledging the Signs ... 104
    Growing from Failure 107
    Becoming a Mature Adult 111
    Signs of Functionality 116

Chapter 8: Forgiving Yourself. Forgiving Others 120
   Forgiveness Can Be a Challenge 124
   Myths About Forgiveness 126
   Means Towards Forgiveness 130
   Being Kind to Yourself 134

Conclusion 137

References 139

Introduction

Your mindset is standing in the way of you being able to change your thoughts. If you are tired of feeling disappointed and incapable, there is no better time to make the necessary changes to the way you think. The wounds of your past have been holding you back from achieving your current goals. If you feel that you keep putting in time and energy, only to be met with disappointment, you are not alone. Whether it is past trauma or complicated family relationships that you are dealing with, anything that is impactful can take you off course. It is natural to feel that you will never find your way back, only navigating through your days to feel that you are barely surviving.

With the help of methods that truly work, you will be able to reclaim your thoughts and heal yourself. Everything you do from this moment on will be for the better. There are many external factors that you cannot control. They can be so overwhelming sometimes that you feel you need to continually make everyone else happy. In the process, you might forget about your own happiness. By reading this book, you are taking back this control. The focus is now set on what brings you joy and how to make it last.

Providing you can relate to these statements; you likely experience negative thoughts that hold you back. Not only do your negative thoughts influence your decision-making abilities, but they also do their best to keep you from making any progress. When you believe you are not enough, you will not have a reason to move forward. Instead, you will find yourself stuck in repeating cycles that feel very difficult to manage. When there is not much to look forward to, seldom going to be a reason to make a change. You must want to make changes for yourself and your happiness.

Another issue you may be dealing with is the inability to let go of your past. It is no secret that your past can haunt you for a very long time. While you are not solely made of past events you have lived through, these experiences still shape you to a certain degree. Being unable to let go of and heal from these experiences fully will keep you from thriving in the present. Since you are so focused on the past, whether consciously or subconsciously, there is little room left to enjoy what is going on right in front of you. Some fears have likely carried over from that time, hindering you and preventing you from taking risks.

When you are living this way, your daily routine becomes a lot harder, and so do the interactions you have with others. What is supposed to be enjoyable and comforting is more likely to feel stressful and unmanageable.

It is hard to feel that you can relate to others when you are suffering from residual insecurities, convincing you that things are not going to be okay. Nobody deserves to live this way, yourself included. Tell yourself this as you work on turning your life around for noticeable improvement. Understand that you have the power to change what you dislike and to live in a way you are proud of.

After reading this book, you will be able to:

Realise you can change for the better

Transform your negative thoughts

Deal with your problems

Finally let go of your past

See yourself from a different perspective

Get ready to uncover different methods for keeping yourself happy and making your days feel manageable again. Several factors try to strip this security away from you, but you will be able to hold on to it for good this time. You will not only make amends with your past but feel more capable of handling any future issues that come your way.

If this sounds like something you are ready for, I encourage you to take the leap. My name is Mini, and I am from London. Throughout my journey, I have been through my fair share of difficult circumstances. I know how exhausting these events can be when you feel you are constantly worrying about the stressors going on. Each day that went by, my life started feeling harder to manage. As everything added up, I became very discouraged that I would be able to live happily again.

Not only can I sympathise with your problems, but I can empathise with them because I have been there myself. I understand that you are going through a tough time, but know it will pass. I am going to help you turn towards your core beliefs to guide through your struggles. By setting proper boundaries and examining your daily habits, you will be able to determine what is working for you and what is holding you back. Through the beginning of a mindful journey, you will discover a brand new approach to self-healing.

The knowledge I have gained during my own journey has taught me what it takes to overcome struggles and to fully heal. It is time to start rooting for a better way of life that is happier and more fulfilling. In this experience, you will begin to realise your self-worth. You will also be able to feel loved once again. I wrote this book to empower you in the way that I found empowerment. I want to share my methods and the steps I took to get here. Through healing, you will learn to accept what happened to you while deciding that you are ready to see what else life has in store for you. Motivation is very important, so don't give up. We are just getting started.

REMEMBER... All steel must bend, all colours must blend, all hearts must break, and all chapters must end.

KEEP IN MIND... Mistakes can make you grow, don't have the constant fear of making one. Never let the fear of failure consume you.. *Remember that, just remember that*

Chapter 1

Core Beliefs—We Are Our Choices

Whatever you believe about yourself on the inside is what you will manifest on the outside.

—John Assaraf

The core beliefs you maintain are deeply rooted assumptions that underlie the way you live. It can have an impact on the way you think, feel, and view the world. Understandably, they can also influence the way you interact with others. Talking to someone with opposite core beliefs can prove to be challenging because this will directly oppose the views you keep. It is interesting to determine what your core beliefs are and how they impact you. Without you even knowing it, your core beliefs might be holding you back from living happily because they are so deeply rooted in your subconscious. Those who grew up in unstable households or have been through unhappy relationships might have experience with adopting core beliefs unintentionally.

Your aim is to identify the beliefs that are damaging and difficult to manage. When you discover exactly who you are as a person, you will be able to pick up on any negative patterns that might be holding you back. It is through negative thought patterns that you unknowingly break yourself down. You might think you are living to the best of your abilities, only to realise that you are damaging your self-esteem and self-worth in the process. That habit stops now. You can find ways to replace it with practices that will better suit your needs.

Our Personal Core Beliefs

The first step to shifting your core beliefs comes from identifying them. To do this, you must get a grasp on the thoughts that are currently in your mind all day. What are they and where did they come from? There are a few easy ways to focus on them. The first is by sitting alone in a quiet room and observing what comes to mind. Another way is to take note of when your mood suddenly changes or shifts. Ask yourself why this happened and what triggered it. Once you identify all of these thoughts you are having, see if you can figure out where they stem from. What underlying event taught you to feel this way? Without changing what you believe, simply observe your findings. The following questions are helpful to ask yourself during this process:

What does this say about my situation? What does it mean?

What does this thought tell me about how I view the world?

What is the worst thing this thought may indicate?

What thoughts do I have about myself that would worsen this situation?

Now, think about your childhood. The way you grew up definitely shapes the way you form your core beliefs. You develop these ideas when your mind is open to learning and growing. Based on who raised you and who you spent the most time around, this will also prove to be an important influence. During your childhood, you discovered who you are as a person because of what you were told. If you grew up hearing you were smart and talented, this is likely what you believe now. Not being complimented or praised enough might lead you to some opposite beliefs that challenge your self-confidence.

Your caregivers also told you how you were to view other people around you. If you were well-socialised as a child, you could likely see the good in people today. You might believe that most people have good intentions. If you were sheltered at a young age, your lack of exposure might lead you to believe that others are inherently bad.

The final piece of the puzzle comes from the way you view the world. If you were given many opportunities as a young child, you might see the world with adventure in your eyes and ambition in your heart. If you were not as fortunate, the world could seem like a scary place to you now.

The Downward Arrow Technique

To shift your negative beliefs, you can use a popular technique known as the Downward Arrow. It helps you to get to the bottom of your core beliefs that were learned at a young age. With this information, you will be able to make the necessary changes to improve your outlook.

Starting with the example of you not getting a job promotion that you applied for. Imagine that you react by thinking, "Of course, I didn't get it".

↓

After taking note of your reaction, you might realise that not getting this job has made you feel sad and angry for days. Imagine asking, "What does this thought say about me?"

↓

You might conclude that your train of thought says, "I never get the jobs I want. I always end up in second place".

↓

You would then ask yourself, "What is the worst part about not being selected?"

↓

With some exploration, you realise that you feel you aren't good enough deep down.

↓

After this, ask yourself, "Why is this so upsetting to me?"

↓

You see that you are in a mindset where your core beliefs tell you that you are not worthy of a better job.

↓

In the final stage of this technique, you realise that your underlying core belief is, 'I am not worthy'.

This technique requires introspection, but it can uncover a lot about the way you view yourself. Now you know what you must work on and what needs to be reversed about the behaviour you learned as a child. These are underlying messages that you send yourself at all times. When you are more aware of them, you will be able to see how they might be damaging.

You can work on changing your core beliefs by changing your perspective. Take a look at your core beliefs from many different angles. How would you react if your best friend felt the same way as you feel? Would you encourage them by telling them they *are* good enough? Seeing your own beliefs from a new perspective can help you feel inspired to make a change.

Now is your chance to experiment. Try adopting views that you have never considered before. If something challenges one of your core beliefs, try to see things from that perspective. Ask yourself how you would react differently if you had different beliefs. See what the pros and cons are of changing your core beliefs.

Negative Core Beliefs: The Childhood Connection

Once you have a better understanding of your core beliefs, you can focus on shifting them. Since they stem from childhood, they can be very prominent driving forces behind all of the decisions you make. To make progress with this, you need to also identify what your triggers are. Your triggers remind you of your negative core beliefs, putting you into a detrimental mindset. For some, triggers can be something that mimics a past event, or they can be entirely unrelated. Your triggers are very personal to what you have experienced. Gently observe yourself and what happened right before you got into a negative thought pattern.

Another element to look for is your lifetraps. These are patterns that begin during childhood that extend into your adult years. Some examples include the need for safety and fear of abandonment or the need for emotional connection and difficulty with emotional deprivation. These lifetraps stem from experiences you had as a child. If you were neglected or mistreated in any way, this is naturally going to lead you into some negative lifetraps. Even if you weren't deliberately mistreated, your upbringing is going to shape these things. For instance, your parents might have never given you any praise, even when you know you did a good job. This creates a suggestion in your mind that you are not good enough.

Not all patterns that you hold onto are going to be negative, but when identifying the ones that are, you must be aware of why they are harmful. Think about the actions that you take to maintain your lifetraps. If you have an emotional deprivation lifetrap, you might seek out partners who are emotionally unavailable. When you do things like this, you are setting yourself up for failure. You must find ways around your negative lifetraps by replacing the damaging behaviour with behaviour that better suits you.

To fully heal from your negative lifetraps, you need to use evidence to disprove your theories. In the past, if you felt that you were unlovable and would be abandoned by your parents, you need to take a look at what is actually going on. Were your parents deliberate about their disapproval of you or were they sending you subconscious hints? Did they treat you well? Focus on these concrete facts as you attempt to unravel what happened to you.

As you hold onto these past traumas, they can prevent you from getting close to people now. When you begin a romantic relationship, your fear of abandonment that stemmed from childhood might get in the way of letting the other person in. If you can disprove your lifetraps, you will feel a lot better about finding ways to finally let them go. In doing so, you are not only going to find inner peace, but you will also be able to improve your relationships.

Current Core Beliefs Become Habits

Through societal pressures, you might feel the need to maintain your current core beliefs, even if you understand they are not good for you. Some beliefs come from your geographic location. Depending on where you reside, you might have grown up with certain core beliefs that were instilled in your upbringing. Since these are so deep-set, it can be hard to look outside of them. It is often when you go elsewhere that you might realise other people have different core beliefs. Sometimes, this can be surprising.

Another significant factor is religion. If you grew up believing in a particular religion, your core beliefs likely came from your studies. Going to a place of worship on a regular basis has placed these ideas in your mind. When you were around so many like-minded individuals, it felt natural to accept these beliefs as your own. There is also the influence of your family members to consider. Similarly to religion, the beliefs of your family members were taught to you at a young age. Since you were always around these people, it is natural that you would adopt their beliefs as your own.

Getting into different friendship circles also influences your core beliefs. As you find people that you can identify with, it creates a sense of solidarity to conform to these beliefs. It is a naturally occurring event that tends to happen, both in childhood and adulthood. A particularly influential time is your teenage years. When you are a teenager, you likely have a different group of friends than you had in primary school. There is also a lot of confusion and changes surrounding the idea of forming your own identity. Sometimes, it is easier to go along with the beliefs of your friends because they are already established.

Keep in mind that your culture also influences your beliefs. Your culture is a part of your beliefs from the very beginning. It encompasses the language you speak, the food you eat, and the beliefs you grow up with. Culture has a huge influence on your upbringing, and it can be enforced by your family, friends, and neighbours. These are the beliefs you do not think twice about because they are such a big part of your life and always have been. You likely have beliefs about when is the right time to start a family, what jobs are considered successful, and which neighbourhoods to live in, all based on your cultural beliefs.

The main reason why these beliefs can hold you back is that you are likely to have the mindset that you mustn't change them. Even if they start to impact you negatively, you are not going to be able to see the connection between your unhappiness and your core beliefs. You might constantly seek approval from people who do not value you. This will always lead you to disappointment and the impression that you are doing something wrong. Since they do not have your best interest at heart, this is not an accurate perception of who you are.

By becoming more aware of this factor, you can make a lot of positive changes. Change can be terrifying, but sometimes, it is necessary. Challenge yourself to take a more in-depth look at how your core beliefs are impacting you. Ask yourself if there are any beliefs that you would be willing to evaluate in order to live better.

The Good vs The Bad

If you are still unsure about what the difference is between 'good' core beliefs and the 'bad' ones, you can compare some of them below. This will give you an idea of whether you share some of the most common core beliefs. You will also discover some negative core beliefs that are holding you back. Keep in mind that these beliefs might not directly align with your own, but you should be able to relate to some of them.

Good Core Beliefs or Commonly Experienced Beliefs

Hurting others is wrong.

Love is good.

You should try to help others in need.

You should brush your teeth daily.

You need an education.

It is good if you have a successful job.

Raising your voice at others is not good manners.

Stealing is wrong.

You should be nice to people.

Lying is bad.

Most of these core beliefs stem from what an average society would agree on. No matter where you live or how you grew up, you can likely identify with a majority of these because they were what you were taught from a young age. These are the societal 'norms' one would expect. While you might not agree with every single one of them, they are arguably the foundation for the good core beliefs you keep.

Bad Core Beliefs or Negative Assumptions

I am ugly.

I am stupid.

I am not enough.

I will not amount to anything.

My happiness does not matter.

I am a pessimist.

Everyone will leave me in the end.

Everyone wants to use me.

The world around me is evil.

Others are inherently bad.

As you can see, these beliefs stem more from a self-deprecating place. When you believe in these things, it is likely that something happened to you that impacted your self-esteem. Since you think you are not worthy of the same love and happiness as others, you are going to continue with this negative self-talk in everything you do. Getting past this kind of negativity can be challenging, especially when you believe that these things about yourself are true.

The way you perceive yourself is going to influence the way your core beliefs develop. If you were taught that you were not good enough for any reason, this message would often stay with you throughout your life. Every time you do something or say something, you likely have a lingering thought about not being enough or that you lack something that others have. It can become a very isolating feeling, destroying your self-esteem and pushing you away from those you care about.

With these beliefs, you likely noticed a pattern. Most of them began with 'I' statements. These are the ones you need to pay close attention to, as they directly affect how you see yourself as a person. It is a lot easier to be critical of yourself than to be kind to yourself. When you put yourself down, you are also opening the door for others to put you down. By reinforcing the behaviour, you are sending other people messages that they can say what they want to you and about you. Challenging these negative beliefs will help you to regain some integrity. The process will remind you that you are more than these thoughts and assumptions.

Be careful of the negative core beliefs that come disguised. For example, if your relationship has come to an end, you might say, "They never cared about me anyway". This can translate to the fact that you believe you are unlovable. These supporting beliefs continue to reinforce your core beliefs without you even realising it. This is why it can be so hard to change the pattern. What seems like a simple fix is a lot more intense than you are anticipating. This does not mean it is impossible though. With more awareness of how you treat yourself, you can adjust the negativity that holds you back.

Shifting Your Negative Thought Patterns

If you find yourself with negative thought patterns throughout the day, you are not alone. According to science, this has to do with your cortisol levels. Cortisol is known as the stress hormone. You can think of it as an alarm system that exists internally. If you are under a lot of stress, your body will create cortisol as a response to help you cope with it. While both cortisol and dopamine (the happy chemical) are chemicals in your brain, cortisol tends to flow more freely. This can easily create negative thoughts and feelings. Since cortisol is released when you are under stress, your brain loves it because it sees it as a form of security. If an abundance of cortisol gets released, your brain is still going to welcome it. Unfortunately, this can lead to severe negative thinking.

As an example, imagine you are driving to work during rush hour traffic. You are already feeling anxious because you do not want to be late. At an intersection, you see a car run a red light, narrowly avoiding an accident with an oncoming vehicle. This is enough to trigger your stress levels. Seeing this almost-accident makes you nervous enough to tell your brain that you need cortisol. Once it is released, you feel less anxious, but the negativity might stay with you throughout the day. When you are asked to take on some extra work from one of your peers, your stress activates again. This releases more cortisol and negative thoughts. You might take on an attitude, clashing with your co-workers. In doing so, you have a negative experience at work.

With biology working against you, there is also the mental factor to consider. You might be feeding yourself self-defeating beliefs. When you think this way, you are setting yourself up for failure or dissatisfaction. There are two main categories that these beliefs fall into: interpersonal and intrapersonal. Use the table below to differentiate the behaviours.

Interpersonal	Intrapersonal
Blame	Perfectionism
Submissiveness	Approval
Fear of Conflict	Achievement

Each one of these beliefs can work against you negatively. This is not to say that feeling this way is inherently wrong, but you must make sure to monitor how much control each one has over you. It is best to clear your mind regularly if you feel that you are being overwhelmed by negativity or self-defeating beliefs.

This can be done by staying busy. When you occupy your time with productivity, you will not have time to idly sit around and worry. The instant you stop being productive, this allows you the chance to overthink. Even if you do not have many chores or responsibilities to tend to, keeping yourself busy with a hobby can result in the same positive experience. When you can concentrate on a task and keep your hands moving, this will change the way your thoughts form. By the end of your experience, you will feel proud of your accomplishments.

You can use physical strategies to break through your negativity. When you worry a lot, you become tense and uncomfortable. It is healthy to improve your circulation often. To do this, lie down on the floor or another flat surface. Roll over onto your stomach, and return to the position on your back again. This movement will promote blood flow, improving your circulation. It might seem silly to roll around on the floor, but the exercise stems from a form of worship known as Shayana Pradakshina. This has been practised for centuries in ancient cultures.

When negativity strikes suddenly, you might not always have the time to roll over to restore your circulation. A quicker action you can take that you can do almost anywhere is shaking your hands out. Imagine the negativity leaving your body as you shake your hands. Feel the relief entering your mind. This trick works in a physical manner as well as a mental one. Envisioning the negativity leaving helps you to convince your mind to feel at ease.

Become a witness to your thoughts, even when they are unpleasant. If you are only trying to avoid them, they are bound to come back, and they may even be more powerful. After each thought you have, try to experience it. Discover its true meaning, digest the information, and then let it go. This might leave you with some work to do and ways to heal yourself. Make sure you are up for whatever is necessary to return to your peaceful mindset. Being happy does require work sometimes, but it should never be debilitating. When you become a witness to your thoughts, you are taking away their potential negative power.

When your mind tells you that you are unworthy or not good enough, reframe the sentences that are forming. Instead of believing that you are 'never going to be enough', think about this statement as a potential for improvement. While there isn't something you can do right now, what are the steps you can take to become better? Forward-thinking tends to stop worry in its tracks. If you can find a solution to the problem you are facing, this will bring you peace. If you feel that there is someone better than you or smarter than you, don't feel like you will never get to their level. It takes work to get there, but if you are willing to focus on the work instead of the defeat, you will soon see yourself as an equal.

Chapter 2

Deep Breaths, Less Stress— Be Mindful

Your strongest muscle and worst enemy is your mind. Train it well.
—Ganesh Laulkar

A tool that many overlook, mindfulness can help you succeed. To be mindful, you must have an awareness of what is going on at all times. Not only should you pay attention to the external factors that happen to you, but also your choices. When you are mindful, you are better able to understand situations that occur. This gives you more flexibility to cope with what is going on in life. Some people struggle with mindfulness because it is a lot easier to simply focus on what is happening to you. Your feelings and emotions can take over, making you oblivious to your surroundings. Through mindfulness, you will learn how to accept what you cannot change and adapt to become the best version of yourself possible. Know that your mind is one of the strongest tools you have, as long as you know how to use it. As soon as it starts to work against you, it can turn into your worst enemy.

To better understand how to be mindful, consider the last time you fully paid attention to what was going on around you. The art of paying attention on purpose is the basis of mindfulness. When you live this way, it becomes a wonderful habit that can lead you to many new discoveries about who you are and why you feel the way that you do. To adopt this habit, you must align your mind and body. This means, if you are feeling good mentally, you should also be taking great physical care of your body. When you can accomplish this, you will be ready to pay attention to what is going on around you. If there are any discrepancies between your mind and body, they tend to form distractions that you will focus on instead.

Turning off auto-pilot is one of the hardest things to do. When you go through the same motions and habits each day, it is natural to just do what you have always done. This isn't going to result in a change though. To transform your mind and the way you think, you need to become more aware of the choices you make. The art of mindfulness develops as soon as you reclaim the way you are living. Instead of making small talk with those around you, try to get to know them. Eat something new for lunch. Make deliberate choices and take deliberate actions.

A common misconception about mindfulness is that it is religious. Many people do not want to participate in it because they believe it has to do with a form of worship, but this is not true. While many religions boast the practice of mindfulness, it is simply a tool that you can use to realign your life. It can be practised by those who are devoted to religion or by those who do not identify with any particular set of beliefs. Another misconception is that mindfulness is the same as meditation. You do not have to stop and close your eyes to practice mindfulness. It is an active habit to adopt that influences you on a daily basis. No matter what you are doing, you can work on ways to make your actions more mindful.

Mindfulness is desirable because it benefits you in many ways. When you are more mindful, you will notice that your stress response is decreased. When you understand what is happening to you, the fear of the unknown doesn't turn into stress. You will also have an increased capacity for compassion, meaning you will be able to understand those in your life better. With this understanding, there is less room for miscommunication and tension. On a physical level, mindfulness doesn't only relax you. It also helps boost your immune system! When you take great care of your mental health, your physical health tends to follow.

The Art of Living Mindfully

When you are first getting started with mindfulness, it can be difficult to tell that you are practising it. The act is subtle but purposeful. To help you create this habit, you can use the following exercises to make sure you are as aware as possible. Give yourself a chance to become fully immersed in these exercises, and pay attention to the improvements they bring to your day.

One Minute of Mindfulness

All you will need for this exercise is a timer and a moment of silence. Set a timer for one minute, and only focus on your breathing for the duration of this exercise. Think of this as your only task. You do not need to judge yourself or worry about what is going on around you. The only thing you should focus on is your inhalations and exhalations. You can keep your eyes open or close them. Do whatever feels most comfortable. After you are through, notice how light and uplifted you feel.

Mindful Listening

When you are listening to someone else speak, there is usually a lot going on in your head. It prevents you from fully immersing yourself in what they are saying. Instead of hearing their messages, you might turn your attention inward. This can be incredibly distracting, especially when you want to make the most of the interaction. The next time you find yourself engaged in a conversation, be sure that your mind is clear. Only listen to what they are saying, not what you want to hear.

Transformational 'Chores'

Every day, there are tasks you must do around the house. Your chores usually elicit some type of negative response because they are little moments where you must focus on doing work. After a long day at your job, doing your chores might be the last thing on your mind. Instead of dreading them, you can turn them into mini mindfulness sessions. When you are folding laundry or doing the dishes, do not rush through the task to 'get it over with'. Do a good job and only focus on what you are doing, not what else you have left to do. After you complete each task on your list, let it go.

Eating with Awareness

When you eat, you are most likely focused on anything else but the food you should be enjoying. It has become a popular habit to turn on the television or grab your phone while you eat. Distracting yourself from your meal makes it seem like a troublesome task that you are trying to avoid. Get back to the simple pleasures of food. As you are eating, appreciate the nourishment you are consuming. Notice the tastes of the food and why you enjoy them. Make sure not to rush, taking appropriate-sized bites to avoid digestive issues.

Slow Down!

In almost every aspect of your day, you rush through each task to get to the next one. There seems to be a constant pressure placed on doing more, being more, and saying more. What happens when it feels like you are never enough? This is a sign you need to slow down. Be present, and you will feel happier. Even with tasks that require deadlines, you must work carefully and deliberately. Do your best to focus on what you are doing, not what you hate about what needs to be done.

One Thing at a Time

Multitasking disguises itself as a time-saver, but it can become a detrimental habit to adopt. When you work on too many things at once, the quality of your actions decreases. For example, if you have to write multiple reports, you are going to lose details when you jump back and forth between them. Work on one at a time, and work in a time-sensitive order. It will allow you to do your best work without sacrificing any quality.

'Watch' Your Mind

When you turn your attention to the art of self-observation, you are automatically going to become more mindful. The instant you realise you are not mindful of your actions, you can gently guide yourself to a new approach. By stepping outside of the continuous stream of expectations and learned habits, you will be better able to make the most of what you are doing and saying. Practice shifting your focus when you feel overwhelmed. Instead of using the same patterns that stress you out, try something new.

Nothing Time

Staying idle is often frowned upon. You are seen as lazy or a failure when you stop to do nothing. Don't let these views fool you—taking the time to do nothing is terrific for your health. As long as you are not ignoring any responsibilities, you deserve a moment to sit down and do nothing. This clears your head, getting rid of any lingering negativity. Sitting outside in the sunshine or your favourite room in the house can be very positive. Enjoy this short time without any obligations, learning how to just 'be'.

Mindful Walking

This is a mindful action you can take without sacrificing any of your time. You must walk each day, so you might as well make the most of it. When you are about to get up to walk, focus your attention on what you are doing first. Remind yourself of where you are going and how you will get there. As you rise, take even and confident strides. Remain mindful of your breathing and your purpose. As you walk, remember that you are doing so deliberately. Feel thankful for your ability to get around.

Come to Your Senses

Your senses are located under the constant chatter in your mind. When you feel that your head is too crowded, look beyond the noise. Focus on your senses. What do you see? Feel? Smell? What can you touch? Remind yourself of these rudimentary forms of living, knowing that they are all you need. By staying in touch with these actions, you will have the ability to enjoy your life and live in the present moment.

Urge Surfing

There are many times throughout your day when you will experience urges. For instance, you have a craving for chocolate, or you want to stop at a clothing store to take a look around. You might believe you have to resist these urges because they are not good for you or benefit you in any way. Know that urges do not have to be met with a declination or an invitation. You can simply observe what you are craving or desiring without taking any deliberate action. Make a note of this and move on with what is productive.

Practice these actions consistently, and they will become regular fixtures in your routine. Living mindfully does not have to be complicated or challenging, so adding a few of these habits into your day will make a big difference in the way you feel.

Mindfulness Matters

Extending your practice of mindfulness to the way you treat other people has the potential to improve your well-being. Being full of conflict and negativity is not a healthy way to live. It drives others away, causing damaging effects on the relationships you have established. In order to obtain peace in your life, you must work on making these existing relationships (and future relationships) even better. Once you have successfully learned how to listen to your stream of consciousness, you can use your skills to become a better friend, parent, partner, and employee.

If you want to expand your mindful actions, consider taking the following steps to create more mindfulness in your daily interactions. Begin with opening your mind to the idea of all things unfamiliar. When you speak with someone who comes from a different cultural background or upbringing, they are bound to have different world views. Learn from them. Experience the ways in which you are similar and the ways in which you differ. Note that there isn't such a thing as a perfect set of beliefs. Everyone feels the way they do for a reason.

Remind yourself that there is nothing wrong with being different. When someone is different from you, this does not necessarily mean that they hold beliefs that directly oppose your own. Many people mistakenly see differences as conflicts that do not need to happen. Two different views on the same subject can coexist without the need to start an argument. While you might respect the person and their beliefs, this also does not mean you need to change your own. Stand up for what you believe in without putting anyone else down.

Your inner critic can be a harsh voice to hear in your mind continually. Not only will it judge you, but it will also form judgements about others. You can keep your inner critic in check by reminding yourself that harshness tends to be a defence mechanism. What is feeling threatening to you, and why? The next time you feel a judgement forming about another person, ask yourself if this isn't simply a reflection of the way you feel about yourself. Ensure that you are not projecting your insecurities.

Make sure that you aren't minimising the struggles that other people have. Their battles are going to be different from your own, but that is because they are living completely different lives. You cannot compare their issues to your own. It is an unfair starting point. Have some compassion and empathy by simply listening. Most of the time, those who are struggling only want a listening ear. Do not give advice unnecessarily because this can come off as judgemental. If they are seeking advice, they will ask you.

While many things wear you out and make you feel emotionally and physically drained, do not let these things impact your relationships with your loved ones. It is not their fault that you got caught up in traffic or had a bad day at work. Appreciate the love and support you are surrounded with because it might not always be there. Teach yourself how to be present when you are spending time with your loved ones. Do not focus on what is wrong or why you had a bad day. Instead, see the value of each interaction for what it truly is.

Overall, the act of being mindful of other people involves being more patient and more compassionate. As long as you can incorporate these traits into your daily routine, then you are doing your best to be mindful of your interactions. Much like being mindful of yourself and your feelings, being mindful of others is simply the act of paying attention. Many things have the potential to distract you, but this will only happen if you let them. By choosing to stay present in the moment, you will not have to worry about this.

Make sure that you are looking after yourself. If you feel unfulfilled, this leaves more room for you to project that feeling onto the people you interact with. You need to make sure you are taking care of yourself and listening to your needs. You can get what you truly want out of life, and it is through no fault of other people that you haven't accomplished this yet. Stay motivated and continue to take care of yourself to the best of your ability.

Those who are only able to focus on the negativity and point fingers of blame tend to be the people who are unapproachable and hard to speak to. Think about things from another person's perspective—it can be hard to know what to say to someone who is constantly thinking in terms of negativity. If you do not balance the bad by reminding yourself of what you can experience that is good, life will only feel negative.

You can become an incredible influence on other people by leading by example. Show others that focusing on mindfulness is a tool to help live in a happier mindset. When this inspiration is continually flowing, this will result in the infectious positivity that is necessary to keep living mindfully. When you can touch someone's life in this way, you will see that mindfulness makes a real difference.

Being Mindful at Work

Your job is one of the places where you should be trying your hardest to be mindful. Not only do your actions directly relate to your success, but they also have the potential to develop strong connections with influential people. What you do for work is your livelihood, so you should be sure that you are putting the right level of importance on this factor. This does not necessarily mean that you must work hard until you can no longer stand, but that you need to do your best at all times. Even though your workplace is designed for work, multiple built-in distractions can try to get you off track.

In a way, being around others who are working the same job can form a connection of solidarity. This might show you that you need to stay productive to keep pulling your weight. In another way, the idea of being around people can become a distraction. Making small talk with your peers can hold you back from completing your workload. You must understand when you need to tighten up your focus and when you can relax. There needs to be a balance if you want to function effectively.

If you find yourself getting distracted by apps on your phone, websites, or the conversations with your co-workers, you need to tighten up your mindfulness practice. Remind yourself of why you are at work and what your goals are. When you think about how your livelihood depends on how well you perform, you should be able to take a more serious approach. This does not mean you cannot incorporate any fun or joy into your work; however, you must make sure you are completing the essential tasks.

To get better at staying focused, you must make conscious choices. Turn off push notifications. When your phone is continuously going off with notifications, you will probably pick it up and procrastinate. Instead of choosing one time each day to work through all of your emails, break this task up. Start with the most pressing matters first. Get to anything that does not require a deadline after you complete some other tasks. When you switch up the kind of work you are doing, you will be less likely to grow tired of it.

Being at work comes with the potential to encounter stressors. If you happen to feel overwhelmed by stress, try the STOP technique. This technique is an acronym where each letter stands for a specific step.

Stop. When you feel yourself getting too overwhelmed, take a moment to breathe. Pay attention to your breathing, choosing not to focus on anything else for a moment. Feel the sensation of your breath, trying to keep it calm and level.

Take a breath. With a steady inhale, take seven seconds to replenish your lungs. Let the air out for seven seconds. This will make you feel calmer and recharged.

Observe. Take note of what is happening to you. No matter if it is good, bad, or neutral, become aware of your surroundings and what is making you feel this way.

Proceed. After you feel that you are calmer and better able to handle the situation, continue what you were doing. Maybe you can take a new approach that will allow you to act more efficiently or effectively.

The way you work with your peers will impact your ability to be mindful as well. If you feel there is a disconnect, suggest having mindful meetings. These meetings will act as brainstorming sessions for everyone on your team. During the meetings, do not allow anyone to be on their phones or computers. Undivided attention is best for making strong connections. Let everyone have the opportunity to speak and express what they believe could use improvement, or what they believe is great about the team. Getting the chance to hear from your peers is a positive way to jumpstart your mindfulness.

In workplace culture, there can often be a competitive feeling that lingers in the atmosphere. While you might be working *with* someone, it can feel like you must work against them. Get this notion out of your mind by realising when you are working towards the same goals. When you can stop believing that this person is a direct threat to your success and is actually for the same cause. You will then be able to complete tasks more effectively.

If you must enter a difficult conversation with one of your peers, try to aim for a solution. Fighting without a solution in mind is what makes it stressful. This causes unnecessary negative energy to linger between the two of you. Conflict resolution skills are a must if you want to maintain a positive working environment. Remind yourself that you don't always need to be right. The better approach comes from seeking a solution when you realise that something isn't working out.

You are allowed to feel frustrated, with both your co-workers and job. Make sure you aren't taking it out on them though. Find outlets to vent your frustrations. Even if you must get up and take a walk around the office to clear your head, this will become a much more mindful approach than lashing out at other people. It will keep the harmony intact and make work a much more enjoyable experience.

Chapter 3

Self-Awareness—
Be Aware of the Present

It takes darkness to be aware of the light.
—Treasure Tatum

You are most likely familiar with the idea behind self-awareness. Still, when asked to define it, the subject gets tricky. How can you be sure that you live your life in a self-aware manner? Everyone boasts that being self-aware is great for you. It connects the way you see your behaviours and the way you realise they impact you and others around you. This is sort of like an extension of your attention to detail. If you are self-aware, you have the capacity to become introspective. You can see things like strengths, weaknesses, ideas, beliefs, responses, attitudes, reactions, and more.

It is thought that being more self-aware is a big step to take when working on your flaws. When you can see things from many perspectives, you might feel more willing to change your ways for growth and harmony. If you often find yourself feeling emotionally unstable or 'triggered', then this is an indication that more self-awareness would be a positive thing. At all times, you should be open to learning more about yourself because there is an endless amount to learn.

When psychologists speak on the topic of self-awareness, they often break it down into two categories:

Public Self-Awareness

This is the type of awareness that becomes apparent when you realise how others might perceive you. Most of the time, public self-awareness comes to the surface when you are put on the spot. Maybe you are giving a presentation at work, or you are telling a story to a group of friends. When the focus is on you, self-awareness usually becomes more prominent. It is in situations like these that you feel the pressure to act socially 'acceptable'. You want to appear normal and desirable to those around you, so you will do your best to play by the rules and participate in cultural norms. In some cases, these situations might give you what is known as 'evaluation anxiety', where you feel nervous about being judged by others.

Private Self-Awareness

This type of self-awareness occurs when you become aware of certain aspects of who you are in a private way.

This might happen when you see your face in the mirror. Only you know what you are thinking at this moment. Forgetting something important is also a good example. When your stomach lurches forward after realising you forgot to take the food out of the freezer to thaw, this is a private moment of self-awareness. It can occur during positive moments too, such as the minute you see your partner and your stomach feels like it has butterflies inside. Certain loved ones might be clued into these moments if you let them. Being vulnerable with someone can give them a glimpse into your private self-awareness.

What Happens When You Lack Self-Awareness?

Life's difficulties increase when you have minimal self-awareness. If you find yourself acting like a bully towards others, this is a projection of your internal feelings. Rather than becoming self-aware to find out what you need, you are taking the emotions and pain out on people who do not deserve it. Being defensive and controlling are two signs that you might need more self-awareness in your life. These traits appear when you are unwilling to take a look at why you are unhappy. Instead, you would rather deflect and distract from these feelings.

Being passive-aggressive is a big indicator that you are not self-aware. By saying one thing and meaning another, you are repressing your feelings in some regard. If you want people to know you are upset, stop telling them that you are "fine" with the intention of them eventually feeling bad for you. Another trait is when you make excuses. These excuses are often used in place of internal observation. When you point the finger of blame on anyone but yourself, this shows that you need more work in the self-awareness department.

The main takeaway is that a lack of self-awareness makes you a less likeable person. Suppose you are continually being harsh to those around you for not understanding you. In that case, you are going to have a difficult time keeping meaningful relationships in your life. This happens because you do not give them enough information to understand fully. You are also going to find it hard to fully accept yourself and love the person you are. Self-awareness connects a lot of positive concepts; it is necessary.

When working with others who are not self-aware, this can pose a new set of problems. Your thoughts and ideas might clash, and the other person will not pick up on the necessary social cues to change their behaviour. This can make for a tense work environment that creates unnecessary stress. It is important to have your own sense of self-awareness so you can better equip yourself with the skills necessary to deal with others who are not quite there yet. Keep in mind that not everyone has gone through a difficult childhood or a traumatic situation. Some people are naturally less self-aware because that is in their personality.

Can You Be Too Self-Aware?

Self-awareness sounds like a great thing, but anything in abundance can turn into something negative. If you feel that you have too much insight on your behaviours, this can lead to some serious second-guessing. It might hold you back from participating in the things you enjoy because you will become fearful that something will go wrong. Everything in life needs a balance to thrive, and self-awareness is no exception to this rule. To better understand how to create this balance, it is important to take a look at another main source of your self-consciousness.

Self-Consciousness

In addition to public and private self-awareness, there is also the element of self-consciousness to consider. Those who are seen as more self-conscious usually have a higher level of private self-awareness than most. Being hyper-aware of how you see yourself can both help and hinder you. On one hand, it can help you correct any flaws in your behaviours. On the other hand, you might use this information against you in a self-sabotaging way. This can hold you back from making decisions you are almost certain you will fail in.

If you are the type who is very privately self-aware, you are likely very secure in your personal beliefs and feelings. They guide you along the way. Since you tend to be so focused on what is going on internally, this means you are also receptive to the negative thoughts and feelings that enter. If you become too fixated on them, it becomes hard to remember the positive ones. Keeping your focus solely on what is negative leads to anxiety and depression.

Another type of self-conscious behaviour occurs when you are more focused on public self-awareness. This can manifest as caring a lot about what other people think about you. For this reason, you might stick to the norms and behaviours you have always known, rarely deviating from this foundation. When you stick to what feels familiar and safe, there is less of a chance in your mind that others will judge you. Those who think this way do not enjoy trying new things. They will go out of their way to avoid them if it means they can stick to their known habits.

This kind of self-consciousness can also lead to evaluation anxiety. You might feel distressed, worried, or anxious that people are judging you, even as you do something simple like walk into a room. This fear can become very debilitating, with the potential to develop into something worse, like social anxiety disorder. It is proven that there is such a thing as too much self-awareness, and this happens when the habit begins to hold you back or make you feel unhappy.

As you determine where you fall in each category, remind yourself that there are differences between self-awareness and self-consciousness. Breaking down the term 'consciousness', it means that you are aware of something external or something that resides within. This can range from your body to your lifestyle. Your awareness begins when you realise that you can act introspectively, separate from everything in everyone else's environment. It magnifies the fact that your way of life and your choices will lead you to different places if you let them.

It gets hard to monitor your levels of each behaviour when you find yourself on auto-pilot. Doing things out of habit or memory takes a lot less work than tuning in because you are feeling self-aware. Without fully realising the power behind your words, actions, and feelings, you might be unknowingly treating yourself (or others) unfairly. Sensitivity is necessary to discover exactly what is going on internally. What is stopping you from being as self-aware as you need to be?

While it is nearly impossible to remain self-aware 100% of the time, there are ways you can improve yourself. By putting in some effort, you will see that you can slowly become more self-aware in every aspect of your life. If you have ever dealt with someone who seems to lack even an ounce of this trait, you might have met someone who has anosognosia. This is a pathological condition that is indicated by a lack of self-awareness. Sometimes, the condition can be related to frontal lobe damage. A lot of common mental illnesses have small elements of anosognosia to them. These include bipolar disorder, multiple personality disorder, and autism spectrum disorder.

The Three Levels of Self-Awareness

The act of self-awareness is much more than placing judgements on your actions. You need to understand the full picture to truly understand your intentions. By observing the three levels of self-awareness, you will be able to decipher your thoughts and behaviours.

What Are You Doing?

> Life is full of painful moments, even when it is going well for you. What does not hurt you physically might end up hurting you mentally instead. Most people want to avoid pain at all costs. They would come up with distractions than open themselves up to the hurt that awaits. By transporting your mind somewhere else, you can momentarily forget about your pain. Habits like picking up your

phone to check out what has been happening on social media, overeating, or drinking too much can become debilitating after a while.

There comes a point when you must become self-aware of your pain. Not only do you need to recognise it, but you must realise how it impacts you. It might even be strong enough to affect those in your life or around you. To become better at dealing with your pain, you need to identify your distractions. These are the things that you would rather do when life feels hard. These distractions aren't necessarily what is best for you.

You might occasionally need an escape from the stressors in life; this isn't a bad thing! Everyone does. What you need to be sure of is that you are choosing your distractions and they are not choosing you. This means you must have control over them, and you are able to stop when need be. This will help to tackle the difficult emotions you come across. How you use your time plays a crucial role in your ability to process your feelings.

What Are You Feeling?

Getting rid of a lot of your distractions can lead you to the realisation that you have a lot of pent-up anger or aggression. After being repressed for so long, it makes sense that your negative feelings would come out at the same time once you let them. If you are one of those people who feel freaked out to sit alone with their thoughts, or to meditate, then you probably have some pent-up feelings that exist just below the surface.

This stage is uncomfortable for most people because it leads to the discovery of who you are as a person. Now is the time to address your emotions, all of them. It isn't going to be easy, and it might take a long time to navigate through everything, but it will be worth it. When you no longer have any emotions holding you back or keeping you from having certain life experiences, you will know you've made the right choice.

The first round of emotions will presumably be the most powerful. These are the ones you've been keeping just below the surface, and they have likely been itching to get out for a long time. Anything underneath them is residual emotion that can be dealt with at a slower pace. Try not to overwhelm yourself by thinking you need to tackle every single emotion at once—that isn't realistic or helpful to your progress.

What Are Your Blind Spots?

During this stage, you might realise that a lot of what you think, feel, and say are merely reactions to situations that are happening at the moment. At your core, you might not actually feel this way. If you had a bad day and you bring this energy home, you are more likely to get into an argument with your partner. It could simply be over what you want to watch on television. This does not mean you have a problem with making this decision or getting along with your partner, but it does show how a prior stressor can linger and impact you.

Stopping this behaviour before it hinders you is important. Instead of taking your feelings out on your loved ones, address them and deal with them personally. Do what it takes to feel at peace. Whether this is self-care or going to therapy, it will benefit you and everyone in your life that you care about.

Ask yourself these questions regularly. When you check-in with yourself frequently, you will become even more self-aware. By becoming more inquisitive about your feelings, you will discover what truly lies in your subconscious.

The Significance of Being Self-Aware

> *"A self-reference walks into a joke. This one".*
> *—Eugene Dubossarsky*
> *(Self-Reference Jokes)*

Start by assessing the way you talk about yourself and the things you think about yourself. This is the basis for your other communication. If you notice a pattern of negativity, this is likely going to leave you feeling like you have low self-esteem or low self-worth. Your thought patterns must change before you become self-aware, or else you will simply focus on tearing yourself down and making yourself believe you aren't good enough.

Take the time to listen to the tone of your inner voice. This should be attempted alone and in a quiet room. Pay attention to the thoughts that come up when you have the freedom to think about anything you want. Do you notice any patterns or habits? Most people who have negative inner voices will usually start by criticising themselves. This might extend to opinions about your personal appearance or things you have done wrong recently. It can be challenging to silence the negativity when it is constantly on your mind.

During this time, do not try to change anything about the way you are thinking. Simply observe what happens. This will give you an idea of the work that must be completed. Chances are, you will be able to focus on things that make you feel positive and happy. Inner thoughts can be incredibly diverse if you take the time to listen to them. Without passing any judgement on yourself, let the thoughts form freely.

Another strategy you can use to enhance your self-awareness is to rely on your senses. In particular, your senses of sight and sound can clue you into how you feel. Through the filter of your self-talk, these senses will spring into action when you must assess a situation. An example of this would be a frown that isn't angry. You might frown because you just realised you forgot to bring your lunch from home. Realise that another person who only sees what is going on externally isn't going to know this. They might look at you, see your frown, and feel too intimidated to talk to you. Just like others should not judge you, the same practice should also be applied in the way that you do not judge them.

The next time you feel judged by another person, take a step back to have a moment of self-awareness. Were you speaking to them, or did they simply walk past you? Is there any body language or attitude they could have misinterpreted? These are interesting elements to think about because, without the internal thought component, other people honestly will not know how you feel unless you tell them.

The final step comes from getting aligned with your feelings. This can be difficult for many reasons because not everybody is comfortable getting in touch with them. Some do not even know how. No matter what stage you are on, try to work with your feelings the next time they arise. If you genuinely do not know how you feel, take a look at any physical inclinations that might help you. For example, if your face is flushed and red, this might indicate that you are angry or embarrassed. The feeling of butterflies in your stomach can mean you are anxious or intrigued. Your body is almost always going to have a corresponding response to help you figure out what you are feeling.

When you put these steps together, you will feel more fully aware of the message you are sending to other people. Remember that your words only make up part of it. Trying to imagine what other people see when they speak to you or look at you will help you to uncover the assumptions that are being made. If you do notice any flaws or weak points, you are now at an advantage where you can correct and improve them. Work on your non-verbal communication and pay attention to the way you treat others. All of this is going to make you a better, self-aware individual.

Social Awareness with Others

> *"Be kind, for everyone is fighting a battle you know nothing about!"*
> —Wendy Mass

To improve your relationships, both romantic and platonic, you need to use your self-awareness skills and become socially aware. This indicates that you have emotional intelligence—that you are aware of how you present yourself and that you have the capability of upholding meaningful interpersonal relationships because of it. Having emotional intelligence and social awareness means being able to take cues. If someone is uncomfortable and wants to end a conversation, you will see them begin to distance themselves from you physically. They might also verbally express that they should get going. If a conversation is going well, the person might come closer to you. They might touch your arm or your shoulder to indicate their comfort level, and their tone will be warm. These are only a few examples of the cues you should be looking for, but they should be easily discoverable with the right amount of social awareness.

Not everyone is going to be easy for you to read. Different personality types create different challenges within interpersonal relationships, but having a strong foundation of emotional intelligence will help you navigate these interactions. The best way to begin is to always pay close attention to what is going on. Whether you are having a conversation or just enjoying one another's company, hear their words and view their body language. This will tell you most of what you need to know. Have you ever been able to tell that someone close to you is upset without them verbalising it directly? You likely found out based on their speech patterns, voice, and body language. This is exactly what happens when you are paying attention—you can uncover messages that the person might want you to know but cannot directly express.

You shouldn't always be analysing other people for alternate meanings in what they are saying, but sometimes, your intuition will tell you that it is necessary. Look for contradictory statements. These are simple inconsistencies in what the other person is saying that might indicate their true feelings. For example, your partner might express that they are okay with you skipping out on date night to hang out with friends. In the same conversation, they might also say that they wish you spent more time together. These statements would contradict, indicating that your partner might not actually feel okay about you choosing to hang out with friends.

Make sure to observe their body language as well. In the same example, your partner might become physically withdrawn after you bring up the idea of skipping date night, even if they agree that they are alright with it. Maybe they feel less affectionate and don't offer to hug you goodbye. These are indications of behavioural patterns that suggest more is being felt than what is being communicated. When you have social awareness, you pick up on these things fairly easily. When someone is acting differently, you will most likely notice.

Above all, you must use empathy to understand other people entirely. Put yourself in their shoes. Imagine what it is like to be in their situation. While you might think you would act differently if it were happening to you, think about the factors that *they* are experiencing. Empathy helps to bridge communication gaps. When you do not fully understand their experience, using empathy can help you find peace with it. You might never fully know what they are going through, but showing them that you are trying will strengthen your relationship.

When you have great social awareness, you are better able to assess a person's character. This means you will be able to identify the traits they possess, both good and bad. With this ability, you should quickly learn if they are going to make a good partner, friend, co-worker, etc. Once you have social awareness, you will also have the chance to understand that many external influences shape people's traits and behaviours. From where they grew up to how their last boss treated them, each person is going through their own unique experience.

The Balance Between Social Awareness and Healthy Escapism

Being around other people can be difficult for those who are introverts. This happens because introverts need time alone to recharge. They might enjoy being socially active with those around them, but it can still feel exhausting. There are moments when you might want to seek out a form of escapism. You cancel your plans or shut off your phone to avoid being contacted with social propositions. Healthy escapism does exist, and you must figure out ways that work best for you so you can fully recharge.

A form of healthy escapism can be something simple that you enjoy doing alone—a hobby, for example. You can sit down and draw or paint for an hour. This will make you feel good, and it might allow you to feel that you can be around other people again. Doing something creative is a way that you can focus your brain on something that makes you feel good but requires no social obligation. Another way you can escape healthily is to take a solo drive—enjoy the sights you see, and appreciate the journey. Here are some other examples of ways you can socially escape in a healthy way:

Work out

Listen to music

Cook a meal

Organise your closet

Take a few photos

Jot down your thoughts in a journal

Go for a walk around the block

Chapter 4

No. It is a Complete Sentence— Stretch Your Boundaries.

Boundaries don't keep other people out, they fence you in.
—Shonda Rhimes

Any relationship you find yourself in requires boundaries. Whether you are romantically interested in someone or working together at the same job, boundaries keep you safe and secure. They provide you with space, both physical and emotional, that is necessary for meeting your needs and staying true to yourself. The boundaries you set also indicate how other people can treat you. They indicate what you deem acceptable and what you believe is not okay. Staying true to your boundaries will prevent you from being hurt or betrayed by people in your life.

Think of your boundaries as lines that divide the property. When you live in a house with a garden, your space is separated by a fence, a boundary. Ideally, your neighbour respects this by keeping his belongings on his side of the fence. If he were to store his lawnmower on your side of the fence, this would be an indication that your boundary is not being respected. It would likely cause an altercation between you and your neighbour, and you would tell him that he needs to stay on his side of the line. Mental boundaries work the same way, but they are only effective if you uphold them. This involves telling someone when they are doing something that is not okay by your standards.

Your boundaries keep you true to yourself. They uphold your morals and values, protecting you from what you find unacceptable. Boundaries can also act as a form of self-care. When you stand up for what you believe in, this does great things for your self-esteem. In relationships, they create realistic expectations between you and the other person. Suppose you are looking for something serious and you have a boundary against one-night stands. In that case, your potential partner will not be able to expect that this is going to be something casual. This puts you both on the same page, determining if you will have the right compatibility to turn the relationship into something serious.

What Are Your Boundaries?

To figure out what you are not okay with, you need to be aligned with your personal values. What matters most in your life? What do you prioritise? It is safe to say that anything that threatens your values and morals would need a boundary around it. This means that anyone who enters your life must be respectful of this, either because you tell them upfront or you indicate when they have crossed a boundary. Depending on the scope of your relationship, this might have to happen at the moment. In romantic relationships, this is usually discussed ahead of time.

Think about what you are absolutely not okay with. Once you have a few things, you have a list of boundaries. The more interactions you have with others, the more you might realise you have additional boundaries. This list can change. What you were not alright with a few years ago might feel completely different now, and that is okay. This is an entirely personal process that you must sort through. By paying close attention to the actions of others, this will give you another good indication of whether or not they would cross your boundaries. If their morals and values line up with your own, this is a good sign that you will likely be on the same page.

Boundaries Can Be Difficult to Set

Boundaries are difficult to maintain for a few reasons. Psychologically, these key factors below can contribute to the behaviours that you move forward with. When you are being influenced by one or all of them, you are likely to act in ways that do not follow prior boundaries that have been set.

FOMO (Fear of Missing Out)

The thought of missing out on something potentially fun or interesting can result in a lack of boundaries. Imagine you need to wake up early in the morning for work. It is a long day ahead of you, and you need to complete a presentation. While this might have been a priority before, you hear that all of your friends are going out for drinks. Knowing you shouldn't, yet not wanting to miss out on the fun, you decide to go out anyway. The next morning, you feel scattered and exhausted. This hinders your presentation. Without any boundaries to keep you centred, you might have accidentally cost yourself the ability to deliver what you are responsible for.

It is healthy to consider your options when presented with a choice. While the immediate response might point to going with the option that seems the most amusing or exciting, you must consider its consequences, both immediately and in the future. Set boundaries based on what is best for you *as a whole*. A lot of people forget to consider the future implications of their choices. After this, they are left with a lot of fixing to do.

Perfectionism

The idea that you must be perfect can definitely do a lot to restrict your boundaries. If you would rather feel immense stress than let someone else down, you might be suffering from some perfectionism ideals. While you might have good intentions behind them, they are still going to result in a lack of boundaries. This is because you are not prioritising yourself or your well-being.

People who suffer from perfectionism tend to have high emotional sensitivity. The behaviour might stem from your desire to make everyone else happy, but you need to make sure you don't forget about your own needs and responsibilities. There will be times when your choices should only reflect your well-being. Getting too caught up in perfectionism can lead to obsessive tendencies that are hard to break. Having a balance is necessary, and your boundaries can help you achieve this.

Social Conditioning

Growing up, you were taught certain things about what is deemed acceptable and what is not. This is how your morals and values formed. When seeing it around you constantly, it is understandable that you would not try to question why things are the way they are. In a lot of cultures, women are known as nurturers. It is common to view women as the ones who cook, clean, and care for the household. In modern times, women still do this, and they work jobs simultaneously.

Imagine being a woman who grew up with similar cultural beliefs to what is listed above. This can become very tiring, and it all adds up quickly. If she is with a partner who expects her to do all the work without pulling any weight, she might settle for this treatment based on what she was conditioned to believe. Instead of setting boundaries, she will continue to push herself to her limits, becoming unhappier by the day.

There comes a time when you must take a look at the bigger picture. While all three of these factors might be influencing you, know that your self-worth is also important. The way you feel, and what you personally believe, needs to be taken into account for you to set clear boundaries. Figure out what you stand for and enforce the point.

Boundaries Can Be Fragile

Sometimes, it is easy to tell when your boundaries get broken. If, for example, you've been cheated on, this is a direct violation of a boundary many have relating to loyalty. There are other moments when boundaries are broken subtly. These are behaviours to be aware of. Your boundaries might be disrespected without you even realising it. You need to do your best to protect and uphold them. The following are some common signs that the people around you do not respect you the way they should.

You Justify Their Bad Behaviour: If you're being mistreated, yet you still stand up for this person to preserve their reputation, this is a sign that you are justifying behaviour you shouldn't. If you feel that your boundaries are being violated, it is not on you to fix the problem. You do not need to put up with this type of treatment, no matter who is acting out in what way.

You Always Blame Yourself: Whenever something goes wrong in your life, relationships, or friendships, you tend to be the first to take on the blame. This is very unfair for you. Everything isn't always going to be your fault. If your boundaries were broken, taking responsibility for something on someone else's behalf can become an unhealthy coping mechanism.

You Start to Doubt Yourself: When you are certain that something is wrong, yet someone tells you that it is not wrong, this can lead you to have doubts about your beliefs. In this process, you might let go of boundaries that are important to you. Anyone who respects you is not going to try to change your mind. They will listen to your boundaries and respect them with no questions asked.

Your Decisions Get Disregarded: When you do feel that you must stand up for your boundaries, it can be confusing to get a message that you are in the wrong. People who do this to you want to have control or manipulate you in some way. It is a red flag to be aware of. If you make firm decisions that get disregarded, this is a direct violation of a boundary that you set.

Signs of Poor Boundaries

To do your part in keeping your boundaries firm, you need to know how to stand up for what you believe in. This can be hard, especially when you have been told for so long that your boundaries do not matter. They are important, and you must work on re-learning this. The following are some signs of behaviours you might be participating in that are making it hard for you to set firm boundaries.

You Are an Open Book: When you are willing to divulge any information to anybody, this can send the wrong impression that others are free to make decisions about your life. Be cautious of who you share things with.

You Feel That You Do Not Have a Voice: Every time you speak to someone, you feel that you are being undermined. This is a sign that the power dynamic is unequal. This can definitely lead to your boundaries being disregarded.

People Use You: Being used is not a good feeling. Evaluate your level of openness and figure out why others are being sent this message that you are there to serve them. Remember, it is within your right to say no.

Your Mood Feels Awful: When you interact with others, how do you generally feel? If your default feeling is negative, there is likely an underlying issue that is influencing your interpersonal relationships. You might need to reclaim yourself before you can be a partner, friend, sibling, or employee to someone else.

If you feel that the people in your life are crossing these boundaries, this is a clear sign that they do not respect you. Those in your life do not have to personally relate to the boundaries to honour them. By recognising that these behaviours are occurring, you will be able to see them as signs of poor boundaries and move forward with cutting out toxic individuals from your social circle.

Handling People Who Cross Your Boundaries

When your boundaries are being crossed time and again, you need a plan of action to get them back in line. You might not have a problem with the person who is crossing your boundaries, but it is only right to stand up for yourself. Putting up with mistreatment over long periods is only going to eat away at you and damage you emotionally. There does not have to be a conflict to get your point across.

Do your best to continue to set your boundaries, even if they have already been broken. When someone does not respect them, say something about it when it happens. Again, no conflict is necessary. Telling someone that you are uncomfortable with the behaviour will suffice. Write down any violations of your boundaries and chart how many times it continues to happen. You will be able to notice any patterns this way.

When doing your own personal work on keeping up with your boundaries, make sure that you understand what you are okay and not okay with. If you have any wavering opinions about certain things, try to get to the bottom of them. Your absolute deal-breakers should be clear though. These are the behaviours that you will not tolerate, no matter what.

Some people you come across might not respect your boundaries, no matter how clearly they have been stated. These people just do not have the emotional intelligence or social awareness to uphold these values. You do not need to keep these people in your life. If someone mistreats you repeatedly, this is a valid reason to want to distance yourself from them.

The best thing you can do is detach yourself from the outcome of their behaviours. If they have been disrespecting you for some time, you already know what to expect. Do not take this personally, and keep yourself at a distance as best as you can. There are some cases when it is inevitable that you must interact with or see this person, but you can always keep the contact as limited as possible by taking action on your end.

If necessary, you can cut them out of your life completely. Again, not being respected is an entirely valid reason to do so. When you stop being in contact with those who do not respect your boundaries, you will feel a weight lifted off your shoulders. It is very freeing to know that you will not have to struggle with the emotional trauma that this person brings to your life.

Setting Boundaries with Toxic People

Those who are considered toxic are normally unsupportive, even abusive. They do not care about your feelings or needs, only about what they want and need. Anyone who brings you down and leaves you feeling negative after you spend time with them is toxic to you. This toxicity is not only reserved for romantic partners. This can be a friend, sibling, or even a parent. More than ever, boundaries are required if you must inevitably interact with someone who is toxic.

The steps to set these boundaries will be exactly the same as any other instance, but you must do your best to reinforce them. A toxic individual will not always be respectful of your boundaries, even when they are directly stated. They will push you and put you into uncomfortable situations that you must work your way out of. Before it becomes emotional and exhausting, you need to distance yourself from this person. If you cannot completely cut them out of your routine, limit the amount of time you spend together.

When they try to undermine your wishes, explain to them that their behaviour is impacting you negatively. This might result in a defensive protest or some other kind of lashing out, but standing your ground is really important. When you sit back and let a toxic person cross your boundaries consistently, this reinforces the message that you are fine with it. In their eyes, it is like you are giving them permission. While you cannot always get through to people like this, what matters most is that you aim to protect yourself. Don't put yourself in a bad situation because you are scared of hurting their feelings.

Healthy Family Boundaries

The idea of setting boundaries with your family might seem strange, especially if you grew up as a tight-knit group. They are no exception though. Anyone at any time can cross a boundary, and that doesn't make it right. Your family knows you very well, but that does not mean they should automatically get to mistreat you. When choosing your approach, it makes sense that you would want to be considerate of their feelings. You do not have to initiate conflict to get your point across. Instead of lashing out or using harsh words, come from an approach of wanting to share your feelings. Explain what having these boundaries crossed feels like. Many families might not realise that it is possible to cross boundaries in this way.

After you bring awareness to the situation, you might be faced with some questions. This is a good sign because it means that your family wants to understand you better. No matter what is going on, always remember that saying "no" is an appropriate response. When you say 'no', you are indicating that you are not okay with what is going on. No follow-up is needed, and anyone who respects you is going to stop what they are doing. Many of us feel nervous to say this to our family because we were taught that it isn't polite. You don't need to be harsh or rude when you say it though. Saying 'no' is one of the easiest ways to stand up for yourself when your boundaries are being crossed.

It is okay to use consequences when setting boundaries with your family. You can explain that if what is going on does not stop, you will have to leave the room or hang up the phone. These non-threatening actions show that you are very serious about the matter. Once they realise where you stand, they should be able to follow suit. It is okay to require time to think about what you'd like to do, seeing that your family might mean a lot to you. There are times when they truly do not know they are crossing your boundaries; it is up to you to decide if you'd like to forgive them and move forward.

If you have never stood up for yourself in this way before, their reactions might be unlike what you expect. Don't take it personally. They are trying to process what is going on, just like you are. While it might be new and confusing, it is not necessarily negative. Setting healthy boundaries for anyone in your life to follow is really important. This is what will keep you feeling safe and happy. Be aware of any boundaries you have been crossing with your family members. Evaluate your actions and their body language, checking in with them regularly. It is possible to maintain an incredibly close relationship still while respecting boundaries.

Healthy Relationship Boundaries

You share everything with your romantic partner, but this does not mean that boundaries are obsolete. To have a great relationship, you need to have them. These boundaries tell your partner what your expectations are and pave the way for how you want the relationship to unfold. If one gets broken, it feels like a betrayal, which is why it is essential to make them as clear as possible. It does not have to feel like a punishment when you decide to set the boundaries in your relationship. Think of it as a time-saving habit that will make your intentions very clear. It is much better to realise that you and your partner are not on the same page early on rather than years later.

You might be wondering what boundaries are acceptable while in a relationship. Jealousy and attraction can fuel you in a way that might come across as unfair. While you want your partner all to yourself, there is a difference between not wanting them to hang out alone with their ex and not wanting them to hang out with anyone else except for you. When it comes to setting relationship boundaries, you need to be sure that you are coming from a place of love and not acting on any insecurities. To assess the state of your relationship, take a look at the table below.

Healthy Expectations	**Unhealthy Expectations**
Knowing you are responsible for your own happiness	Only feeling happy when your partner puts in an effort to make you happy

Having friends that exist outside of your relationship	Relying on your partner to be your romantic partner and only friend
Having open and honest communication	Speaking in a manipulative or controlling way
Agreeing to disagree	Feeling jealous when things don't go your way
Asking what your partner wants and needs	Being unable to express what you want and need
Accepting endings	Being unable to let go

To set effective boundaries with your partner, never assume that you know what they are thinking or feeling. Wait until they tell you. This will prevent any miscommunication from taking place. Once you both know where the other person stands, have open and honest communication about what is expected in the relationship and what is not okay. By giving each other the chance to express this, you will never have to assume what is wrong and what is right. It is a direct and healthy form of communication.

Once you set boundaries, follow through with them. Whether your partner forgets or does not take them seriously, remind them. If they are doing something that directly violates a boundary that you have set, a simple reminder should not start a fight or an argument. At the same time, you must also hold yourself accountable. If your partner expresses that you have crossed a boundary, you need to have more awareness. Prove to them that you are listening and that you value what they are requesting by matching your actions to your words.

Healthy Professional Boundaries

Boundaries that you maintain in the workplace are just as important as any other. When you have a healthy work environment, this will prevent burnout and stress. There are many ways to enforce professional boundaries with your co-workers without coming across as confrontational. When you are a stronger team, you are also better able to provide the best service for your clients. The following are some strategies you can use to ensure you are keeping up with healthy professional boundaries at work:

Keep your home life/personal life to yourself. When you are at work, you should only focus on discussing work and work-related matters with your co-workers.

Use professional language. There is a time and place for letting your full personality shine through, but you might have to dial it down while you are at work.

While you are on the clock, you should not be taking on personal matters. For example, if you got into a fight with your partner before you left the house, you should not be sneaking off to the break room to call them to mend the relationship.

When it comes to your clients, do not go out of your way to buy them gifts on your own or accept personal gifts from them. This keeps your relationship professional.

If someone ever crosses any of these boundaries, stand up for yourself. Mention directly that you are not okay with the conversation or that you do not want to talk about it. When someone respects you, they will care about crossing these lines. Honesty is always the best policy when it comes to dealing with someone that comes across as too aggressive or prying.

Think of your work environment as a support network—you can rely on this network to better your work experience and to motivate you to work harder. There might be times when you talk to your peers about certain clients to do a better job as a collective, but this should not extend to gossip or to talk bad about anyone. Keeping these boundaries by enforcing them on your own and maintaining the respect of your peers and clients, you will ensure that your work environment is optimal.

Chapter 5

One Moment. One Decision. One Action—Start Today

*Sometimes, we motivate ourselves by thinking
of what we want to become. Other times, we motivate
ourselves
by thinking about who we don't ever want to be again.
—Shane Niemeyer*

There comes a point where you will realise that it is time to change your life for the better. This sounds like a broad statement because it is. Your life is made of so many elements that it can feel overwhelming to understand how you must change them all. The good part is, you can make little changes. By only changing a few things at a time, you will feel less likely to get overwhelmed. As you adapt to each change you make, you will appreciate your tenacity and commitment to healing yourself. This is your journey to recovery, and you need to do what feels right.

You Can Alter Your Life

A heavy topic, improving your life sounds very intimidating. No matter what is going on in your life right now, you are probably used to it, so this brings you a sense of comfort. It can be hard to think about what you would change if you had to do so on the spot. The great news is, you don't. Change can occur gradually. No matter how hard you have already worked on your current life path, there might come a point where you realise it is no longer the best path for you. Things change, and you shouldn't feel guilty for going with the flow.

It is easy to love what you do. You might love certain aspects of your job or where you live. These are the silver linings that make you happy and keep you going. What are you passionate about though? This is something that extends beyond love. Your passion is what you want to prioritise over everything else. Maybe you can't because you are worried about making enough money or upsetting people along the way. Your passion is something that never ceases to call out to you. Most people see what they do and what they are passionate about as two separate entities, but they do not have to be.

When you decide what you are truly passionate about right now, you can work on incorporating more of it into your life. Even if you do not make a career change, you can still find ways to prioritise your passions. Volunteer your time towards your passion; do it as a hobby. Whatever it takes to incorporate it into your daily routine, go for it! Living a life full of passion is going to feel very fulfilling. It makes the mundane tasks of your days seem less bothersome.

If you still need some guidance, ask yourself these questions:

What do I want to change?

How do I feel about my current situation?

How could my life improve?

What needs to be done to achieve my goals?

What is a small step I can take right now?

How long am I giving myself to do this?

What am I worried about?

Brainstorming about making changes can allow it to feel less scary. Even if the change is for the better, it is normal to feel apprehensive about moving outside of your comfort zone. Address all of these questions for yourself until you feel that you have the confidence necessary to move forward. Keep in mind that nothing is going to completely transform overnight. It takes steps to reach your ultimate goals.

It is okay if you want to change your life path, as long as you create a comprehensive plan that will get you there. Many devote most of their lives to a particular field or industry, only to discover that it no longer makes them happy. This is why so many switch courses in universities or start new career paths mid-way through life. It isn't necessary to force yourself to do something just because it is what you started doing. Your preferences can change, and you can still become successful.

If you feel that everything is falling apart in your life or you have been trying very hard with no lasting results, these might be signs that it is alright to move on. Go after something that you know you are more passionate about. Your mind and body will also clue you in when they are unhappy. This can appear in the form of anxiety, depression, headaches, indigestion, and stomach aches.

The first step is believing in yourself, and the rest will follow. Don't put too much unnecessary pressure on your journey, as you are still trying to figure things out for yourself. When you find the right path, you will know. It is that feeling of everything falling into place and a wave of relief washing over you.

Career Changes

Your career is your livelihood. It pays your bills and keeps a roof over your head. Of course, you might feel hesitant to change anything about what you do for a living. Despite being unhappy at your job, security is the main factor that is holding you back from making the big move. When you have a calculated plan, changing your career path becomes easier. Knowing what steps to take, you will see that it isn't impossible.

This eight-step plan will put you on the right path to changing your career. When you know exactly what to do, the task will feel less daunting. Though it will require a lot of calculated thinking, you will be certain that you've made the right decision at the end of the day. No matter what, you cannot let fear hold you back. Tell yourself that you *will* find another job that will pay your bills and that you *can* do something that makes you happy for a living.

1. **Assess Your Likes and Dislikes**: Thinking about your current job, examine what you like and dislike about it. The dislikes are usually the driving force behind wanting to change career paths. Once you identify what it is that is making you unhappy, you will know what changes to make. For example, if you dislike your management, you might be able to work at a different company in the same field. If it is the nature of

your work that you dislike, you might be in store for a bigger change of industries.

2. **Research New Careers**: Before you jump into the application process, do some research! You can accomplish this for free online. Pay attention to the median salary of someone who works in the field you are trying to get into. Consider how much competition there will be around you. Focus on researching careers that consider your passions. See if there is any way to incorporate the two.

3. **Consider Your Transferable Skills**: Even if you are changing industries entirely, you might still have some skills that are suitable for other jobs. Don't let your training go to waste; make sure to include your skills on your resume, so employers know what you have to offer. Some companies might see you as a more significant asset because of the skills you possess.

4. **Training and Education**: If necessary, get educated on the field you are trying to get into. It doesn't hurt to take a class, learn from someone with experience, or prepare yourself for the process. It is much better to be over-prepared than to be under-prepared.

5. **Network**: Talk to people in your line of work. The more connections you make, the more opportunities you unlock for yourself. Attend network mixers and pass around your business card. You never know who might be scouting for new employees. There is a lot of power behind connecting with people.

6. **Gain Experience**: If you cannot manage to land the job right away, volunteer when you can. Getting any kind of experience in your desired field is going to help you once you get the job you are aiming for. Take internships and apprenticeships if you need to. Any experience you gain will become valuable.

7. **Find a Mentor**: Through networking, it is likely you can find a mentor that will guide you through the process. This person should be experienced in the job you desire and willing to have open discussions about it. You can learn a lot from just listening to someone else who has gone through what you are hoping you can achieve.

8. **Be Flexible**: If you find a great job that you qualify for, it might not come with the benefits of weekends off or a perfect schedule at first. You usually have to work your way up to that. You are starting over for a reason, so keep in mind you

need to have a little flexibility when it comes to the small nuances. Don't be so quick to write off a job because it isn't 'perfect'. You will earn privileges the longer you work there.

This process does not have to be sudden or fast. If you realise that you want to change your career, you can take little steps towards the final result that will get you there in time. Making a change like this is something that you have decided to do for yourself, so you are allowed to select the deadline. You have the ability to do this, so be patient with yourself.

Pushing Through the Difficulties

Many people like to bring up the difficulties of making life changes, but it does not have to be all bad. When something is difficult, this does not mean you must be miserable in the process. Anything worthwhile is going to challenge you. It will test you in ways you might have never been tested before. Having a firm foundational belief in yourself is going to get you through these moments. You are already aware that a change must be made, so you are on the right track. Feel proud of yourself for getting to this stage, admitting your desire to live a better life.

When something feels difficult, remember that you have to start somewhere. The most successful people around you did not automatically end up on top, knowing what to do. They had to train, struggle, and worry just like you. This is why having a mentor is especially helpful when you are going through life changes. Knowing that you are not the only person who has ever experienced this kind of struggle is reassuring. Verbalise your worries. Chances are, other people in your life have also been nervous about making life changes. The more success stories you read about, the more inspired you will feel.

Don't be too hard on yourself if you make mistakes that delay your progress. When you are trying something new, you are bound to make a few mistakes—this is how you learn for next time. Perfectionism isn't a realistic goal. When you understand the lessons from your mistakes, you will become a better person in the process. Without being too hard on yourself, you can strategise and figure out what other options you could have taken. Imagine the alternative results you would have been met with. The good thing about making a mistake is that you know one error to avoid in the future. Since you already know that the outcome wasn't the best, you can move onto the next option.

Keep a clear picture in your head of why you are making this change. When it feels like a lot of hard work and difficulties, it becomes easy to lose sight of the end goal. Remind yourself that you are making this change to better your life. Consider the benefits you will receive once you are finally at your goal. Think less about the work that you must still get through and more about the progress you are continually making. If you commit to working on your goals a little each day, this is going to make a consistent dent in your progress.

No matter how long someone has been stuck in their ways, change is still possible. Even if you've been at your job for over 20 years, it does not mean you must continue on as though this is the only option for you. Plenty of people make major life changes later in life, just as they do when they are younger. There is no age limit to wanting to better yourself because what you have is right now. Some things will shape your future, but there is nothing wrong with wanting a better today instead of hoping that things will get better later. Life is not a guarantee, so it is best to make the most of it while you can.

When you decide what you are going to change, commit to it. Make this commitment to yourself and keep your word. As you are going through something like this, gaining your own trust is really important. This is going to encourage you to take more risks and to see more victories. Life can become fairly uncertain when you feel that you are only going through the motions. Seeking change indicates that you have a clear direction for yourself that you know will benefit you. Don't stop believing in these intuitions and ideas that you have; they happen for a reason. Your innermost thoughts can guide you when you are feeling unsure about what to do next.

Proactive vs Reactive Behaviour

Generally speaking, there are two ways you go about handling a situation. Proactive behaviour indicates being as prepared as possible. You are still reacting to what is happening, but you have a sense of grace behind your reaction. When you know that you must drive home during rush hour, you take a proactive approach when you put on an audiobook that will soothe your nerves. Since you already know you will be stuck in traffic for a long time, you are planning ahead for your comfort. A reactive approach would be, for instance, getting road rage or falling into a bad mood because of your temper. The two types of behaviour tend to have distinctly positive and negative traits, respectively.

If you have ever been in an argument with someone and said something you didn't mean, this is a great definition of reactive behaviour. Maybe they did something terrible to you, so your initial reaction was to lash out. This acting-without-thinking behaviour doesn't always work out to your advantage. While it might have felt great at the moment to get your anger out, there is a chance you felt guilty afterwards. This creates an emotional blockage that you must now deal with before you can move on from the issue. It can create unnecessary tension and problems in your life.

As you work on determining your behaviour style, remind yourself that critical thinking will help you in almost every situation. When you can do your best to plan ahead for the bad or unpleasant, you won't be faced with as much of a tendency to become reactive. Being proactive gives you a plan that also gives you security. To apply this concept to the entirety of your life, you must be willing to consider what might happen to you. This extends beyond the amount of traffic you will have to sit through.

Taking a look at your relationship, job, and family life, consider some possibilities that are realistic based on how things are currently going. The more honest you can be, the better. If you can sense that your partner is upset because you aren't spending as much time together as you used to, you can take a proactive approach by making time for them and going out on a date night. It is little instances like this that will help you from falling into any reactive tendencies. Reactive behaviour is almost like a last resort or a panic. When you do not know how to control the situation unfolding, all you can do is react based on your emotions. Proactivity brings logic to the situation.

It does take energy to rise above certain situations, but this must be done if you want to be ahead. There will be difficulties that you will encounter, but you now know how to push through them. Use these skills to see the bigger picture. If you cannot see yourself in a happy or positive situation at the end of your hard work, then you might need to reconsider your purpose. Proactive behaviour always has a positive end goal in sight. This practice keeps you motivated and on track with your life.

If you notice that you are being reactive, you do not have to think of this as a failure. We all get tired sometimes, and for different reasons too. You are only human, and you can only endure so much. Use your reactive tendencies to teach you when you are feeling overwhelmed and when you need a break. They can be really helpful if you are willing to pay attention to them instead of punishing yourself for them. There will be times when you cannot help but be reactive—you are an individual with a wide range of emotions. The issues that make you feel incredibly emotional will be hard to bypass without some form of reactivity. Even if you must express yourself in this way, consider how you can also be proactive at the same time. Seek a solution instead of giving in to the problem.

Beating Procrastination

As you work on making progress, one behaviour can stop you in your tracks. Procrastination comes in all forms, and not only in your professional life. You can also procrastinate on things you would like to accomplish in your personal life. To thoroughly beat procrastination, you need to understand how it impacts your life and why it holds you back. In some ways, it seems like a harmless break that you give to yourself, but there is a difference between regrouping and losing track of your goals altogether.

Write your goals down every day. Keep a list of simple to-do tasks that you want to get done. These simple and short-term tasks might not feel worthy enough to be placed on a to-do list, but seeing them written down will solidify your need to accomplish them. When you have a tangible list of things you must achieve, you will be much more likely to follow through and complete it. Saying that you want to do something or you 'wish' you could do something is only going to result in another day of it not being done.

Give yourself enough time to work on each task. Some things aren't going to take very long, such as walking the dog or starting a load of laundry. You can group these tasks into the same category. Other things like cleaning out your closet and going grocery shopping are tasks that can take over an hour. It would be unfair of you to give yourself 15 minutes to complete each of these things. You need to set reasonable deadlines for yourself so you are not setting yourself up for failure. Take into consideration the amount of time you need and always give yourself extra time so you can stay ahead of schedule. If you know that walking the dog takes 10 minutes, factor in 15 minutes, just in case.

Identifying and getting rid of your distractions is a must if you want to become better about procrastination. For most people, phones and television screens serve as common distractions. They are always around you, always tempting. If you must, turn off your notifications when you are trying to get tasks done. Use phone time as a reward for completing a task on your to-do list. Keep the television off, even if you only have it on in the background. While you aren't intentionally focusing on it, you are still subconsciously acknowledging it. This can hinder the speed or quality of the work that you are putting into each task. It is better to remain focused so you do not have to do any extra work later. Save the television as a reward.

People and noise can also become big distractions. When you start engaging in conversations, you are automatically taking time and effort away from the project you are working on. Do your best to find some alone time to complete your tasks. If this isn't possible, make it clear to those around you that you are working and require a proper working environment. Constant noise and chatter, even if you are not participating in it, is still going to distract you. Your brain can only focus on so many things at once, and you should not be spreading yourself thin each time you have a goal to do.

Using incentives is a great idea! If you finish a few tasks, you can reward yourself with a walk around the block or a piece of your favourite candy. Do whatever you need to do to stay motivated. This type of reward system will encourage you to keep moving through your to-do list. It is not silly or stupid if it helps you complete your tasks. The most motivated people still reward themselves in this way. Part of doing hard work is celebrating your victories, and there are no victories that are too small to celebrate. Acknowledge that you are proud of yourself and that you deserve to be happy.

Chapter 6

Accepting the Bad with the Good

The difference between a good life and a bad life is how well you walk through the fire.
—Carl Jung

Even when you are on the best path for your life, you are still going to encounter unpleasant moments. Life is a constant mix of both bad and good occurrences. What matters most is how you choose to handle them and the attitude you take on. By learning how to accept that the bad is inevitable, you will be able to live your best life possible. Being resilient will get you far. It will show you that everything is going to be okay, even when unplanned events occur. Through acceptance, you will be able to find a sense of inner peace that is incredibly important to maintain.

It is natural to become fearful of acceptance, both from yourself and those around you. There are so many reasons to judge yourself and to put your actions under a microscope, but ask yourself if this is truly necessary. By learning how to accept what you cannot change, you are going to find a lot more peace in your life. The same problem occurs when you cannot accept the reality of a situation. If you mistakenly view something for what it is not, this provides you with a way to avoid reality and to embrace instant gratification. The feeling is only temporary, and that is not what you should strive for.

What is a Good Life?

The definition of living a good life is one of the most subjective topics to consider. What is good to you might not mean as much to the next person. When identifying how you plan on living your best life, you need to take into account the things that mean the most to you. In a general sense, a few lifestyles encompass this theory. You can learn more about them and see if you identify with them. While they might not be the lifestyles that you want to live forever, they will get you started on the right path towards the one that is perfect for you.

The Moral Life

To live a moral lifestyle, you must consider if your actions and behaviours are lining up with your moral standards. These are your own personal beliefs of what you think is 'right'. If someone goes against your morals, this is not a person you would get close to if you were upholding a moral lifestyle. When faced with situations that challenge your morals, you would be much more willing to walk away than to be untrue to who you are. Most people who lead this lifestyle believe that there is a divine purpose for it, a form of acceptance or a reward at the end of life. Many religious people adopt this lifestyle because they believe it is how they must live to get to heaven.

The Life of Pleasure

This lifestyle centres around the things that make you feel good. Sex isn't the only thing that can bring you pleasure. Maybe you enjoy trying new foods or shopping for household goods. A lot of people adopt this lifestyle because they believe that life is too short to be miserable. You should strive for the things you want, bringing yourself as much pleasure as possible. Frequently indulging in what you desire can lead you to feelings of bliss very easily. Be aware, heavy indulgence can also come with disappointment. When something doesn't turn out your way, you might feel like you are being robbed of the pleasure you deserve. There is also a chance that you will become too greedy, only focusing on yourself and the way you feel. It is a fine line between gluttonous behaviour and living the way that feels great to you.

The Fulfilled Life

This lifestyle combines the first two. When you live a fulfilled life, you have everything you need. This means you likely have the basic comforts of living and pleasurable elements in your daily life that make you happy. When you live a fulfilled life, you don't have to do much seeking because you feel content. One downside is a loss of motivation for expanding your goals. Since you are already happy with what you have, it might feel tempting to fall into a rut of laziness.

The Meaningful Life

To live a meaningful life means living a life with a purpose. Commonly, those who have children describe their lifestyles in this way. When you must care for another living being, you always have a meaningful purpose. Nevertheless, there is always a reason to do more and to be better, if not for yourself, then for your offspring. Parents aren't the only people who can live a meaningful life, but finding meaning in other ways can be a challenge. This type of lifestyle requires you to look outside of yourself and your own needs.

The Finished Life

This type of lifestyle provides the individual with the misconception that there is no more to learn, see, or do in life.

Usually, those who are older and have already lived fulfilling lives tend to feel this way. No matter what age you are, there is always more to life. By considering your life 'finished', you are selling yourself short. Many people have lovely new experiences in their later years that they would have missed out on if they had adopted this type of lifestyle. Instead of seeing life as something that has an end date, it is wiser to aim for your purpose at all times, hoping that you can become even better.

Deciphering Destructive Behaviours

What's the difference between a psychologist and a magician?
A magician pulls rabbits out of hats, while a psychologist pulls habits out of rats. (Burton 2014)

If there is one issue that gets in the way of living your best life possible, it is destructive behaviours. Whether you are engaging in them yourself or you are around those who do, these behaviours can present you with many challenges. By having a better understanding of what is considered destructive and what to do about it, you will be able to avoid heartache and disappointment when you are faced with them. Being more aware of them also shapes your own behaviour, reminding you that the way you behave directly relates to the level of happiness you feel.

Lying: University of Massachusetts psychologist, Robert Feldman, believes that lying is tied in with self-esteem issues. When someone feels that their self-esteem is being threatened in some way, a natural response might be to lie to make them feel better about themselves. It is a destructive behaviour because it harbours dishonesty. Someone who lies regularly will end up hurting a lot of people and losing the trust of those around them.

Bullying: When someone chooses to bully another person, it is often an escalatory action. The bully is triggered by something that makes them feel insecure or inadequate. Instead of being able to admit their faults, they take their insecurity out on other people. It goes without saying how harmful bullying can be. When you bully others, you are not taking accountability for your actions.

Stressing: Feeling stressed out is a relatively normal response to situations, but this is only the case when you don't let it go overboard. When you feel stressed, you need to have outlets for these feelings, or ways to unwind. Holding onto this stress and never addressing it becomes destructive. Not only will it eat away at you and impact your mental health, but it can also appear in other ways that harm those around you. If you are constantly feeling stressed out, you might be more prone to lashing out at loved ones, even if they have done nothing wrong.

Cheating: This is a very destructive habit because it always involves other people. When you hurt someone at their expense, this is one of the biggest betrayals of trust. Cheating is also linked to being unable to address the way you feel. Whether you are bored in your marriage or you want to cheat on your taxes to save some money, this behaviour quickly becomes destructive because it is based on dishonesty. More often than not, cheaters are left with feelings of intense guilt.

Gambling: This destructive behaviour does not always have to be performed in a casino. Unhealthy and dangerous risks can be considered gambles. Going shopping when you know you cannot afford to pay your utility bills is a gamble. It is impulsive and risky behaviour that is dangerous to live your life around. When you cannot stop gambling, you will not have any constants in your life; this means no structure. Without this security, you will be more likely to spiral out of control.

Gossiping: Most people do not know or realise how damaging this behaviour can be. When you gossip about someone or something, you are talking without their knowledge. Some gossip can be entirely innocent, like chatting about the new trees your neighbour planted in their back garden. Other times, it can be very damaging, ruining reputations, and getting you involved in drama you didn't need to be a part of in the first place. Be aware of how much you talk about others while they are not in the room. This behaviour can be very telling of your self-esteem. Nobody likes to find out that their friend, partner, sibling, or child is talking about them without their consent. This feels like a major violation, and it damages relationships.

These are the most common destructive traits you must recognise. Even if you feel that an individual is not being intentionally destructive, their actions can still impact you regularly if you are around them enough.

It Is Okay to be Sad

In life, you must remind yourself that it is okay not to be okay. Most people believe that they must live perfect, happy lives at all times in order to be successful. This is untrue because life seldom works this way. There are going to be times when something happens, that can upset you—you are only human, and you deserve the chance to express your emotions. Being sad means that you have things that matter to you. It is an indication of your passion and your determination. While nobody enjoys feeling down, it can sometimes become an integral part of how you choose to move forward. Using your sadness to help you overcome the obstacle is one of the greatest things you can do.

When you are first feeling upset about something, let it all out—cry, vent, and do whatever it takes to release some of the negativity you are holding onto. If you keep the fire inside, it will not go away. This only means you will have to deal with it later. After the initial stage of recognising your feelings, try to get to the bottom of what is causing you to feel this way. If you are upset with your partner, do not stop there with your analysis. What is it that your partner did to upset you? Why was it upsetting? You need to get as close to the root of the problem as you can.

Journal about the issue if you cannot come to a conclusion about what is upsetting you so much. It is normal to be too overtaken with your emotions to be able to identify exactly what is going on. Let yourself write about the topic without censoring anything. This will help you get an idea of what is happening in your head and with your thoughts. At this point, some ideas should be starting to form regarding what you need to do to move forward and to stop feeling sad.

There does not need to be a timeline for how long you are allowed to feel sad, as long as you aren't being destructive in the process. Death is not the only instance where you might feel the need to grieve. It is normal to feel this way about anything in life that you care about. Validate your feelings and be easy on yourself. Combating them or denying them is only going to make you feel worse about yourself. During this time, surround yourself with kind and gentle people that you trust. This will help you feel safe as you navigate what needs to be done to feel better.

Talk to others about how you are feeling. While they might not be able to fix your problems, it can be reassuring to know that you have someone on your side who cares about you. This will give you the strength to build yourself up and try again. When you start feeling a little better, the brainstorming can begin. Think about what proactive steps you can take to make your life happier. How can you fix this problem and make sure you don't end up in the same place again? The answers will not be clear every time, but they are worth the critical thinking it takes to get to them. Value your own feelings as much as you value others'. Try not to be so harsh on yourself as you figure out what your best decision is. The answers won't always be there, but that is the point—life is about learning how to get them and then learning how to apply them.

Acceptance

In life, there are many instances where you must practice accepting. At first, you will need to work on accepting yourself for who you are. By learning how to not be so hard on yourself, you will find a deep connection of love that you can use to move forward in life. When you are happy with who you are, this gives you confidence and the ability to interact with other people. Accepting yourself can be very difficult in many ways, and it happens to be a constant struggle for a lot of people. Know that self-acceptance is entirely necessary, and you should always be striving for it. It will make many aspects of your life feel peaceful and more fulfilling.

Next, you must learn how to accept other people. One of the most challenging lessons is that not everyone is going to think and act the same way as you. Many in your life might have completely different morals and values. Those you choose to become close to can be those you deem worthy of your attention and respect. While someone might be flawed in ways you are not, there are times when you can overlook this aspect and still love them for who they are. This is the basis of most relationships, both romantic and platonic. If your partner, child, or friend does something that you disagree with, your initial reaction is not to abandon them. You learn to accept this, possibly guide them in a better direction, and move forward.

There is another interesting element of acceptance to consider—how other people are going to accept you. While you might have a loving and accepting heart towards those around you, this does not mean people will automatically treat you in the same regard. There are plenty of people in life you will meet that do not like you based on something you say, do, or believe in. This does not necessarily mean you must change your ways, but it does mean you have to put on your best coat of armour some days. If you know that you are a good person, you should not let anyone else convince you that you need to change yourself to fit their definition of a good person.

In romantic relationships, things get more complex. Partners do change for one another, but to do this healthily, both you and your significant other should want it to happen. When someone asks you to change something about yourself that you love, this can cause a lot of conflicting emotions. While part of you might want to do this to please them, another part might feel upset because you are no longer staying true to who you are. You must protect yourself from situations like these because your feelings are valuable. Never let anyone dictate who you need to be if their sole purpose of changing you is to make themselves feel better. It is unfortunate that not everyone has your best intention in mind.

There are going to be things in life that you simply will not like. When they are not detrimental to your health or well-being, another element of acceptance comes into play. You must exercise your patience and flexibility to get through these situations or instances that are unfavourable. Things aren't always going to go your way, but this does not mean you aren't adaptable. Appreciate the views you have, but understand they will differ from those of others. You are going to be faced with many situations in life that you do not want to accept but be assured that you are strong enough to get through them. While they might upset you at the moment, you do not have to live your entire life this way. The unpleasant feeling is only temporary. Once you can accept this, you will be able to find a way to move forward. Getting stuck in a rut where you feel stubborn can hold you back. Avoid doing this by reminding yourself that acceptance is a part of growth.

Instant Gratification

When you are working on accepting the obstacles you encounter, you might be quick to gravitate towards instant gratification. This feeling stems from anything that gives you a quick boost of happiness or positivity. It can sound very freeing, but it becomes a problem because it is only temporary. When you make your decisions based on what is going to make you feel instant gratification, you might not be living in a way that provides you with a great future. Living moment to moment can only go on for so long. After a while, the instant gratification is going to wear off, and you will feel as upset as you did when you started—in some cases, worse. It can take a lot of time to learn that instant gratification isn't the best concept to live your life around.

For children, it is very normal to live this way. You see a toy, and you want to play with it immediately because you know it will bring you joy. Beyond this toy is a game that is much more entertaining and lasts longer. You will not see this as a better option because it requires more time to set it up and to learn the rules. Therefore, you select the toy because it promises instant gratification. You are expected to outgrow this theory as you get older. While you are a teenager and a young adult, you might still experience select instances where you choose the instant gratification option over something that is certain and lasting.

During adulthood, you get put to the test because you are constantly faced with options that offer instant gratification. For the most part, you should be able to see that they are not worth it. For example, going out for drinks on a work night is not worth the hangover you will feel when you wake up in the morning. While the drinking promises to be a great time, you need to weigh the risk with the reward. You can drink on the weekend instead, not depriving yourself of the social time you have with friends.

As you consider the choices you make in your life, make sure you aren't only leaning towards the ones that provide you with instant gratification. You must consider your future too. While these decisions might not seem as fun upfront, they will provide you with things the others can't, like lasting security. When you have your life together, this is a great feeling. You won't be tied down to negative emotions and unaddressed problems. There are pros and cons to every decision you make. It is a wise idea to consider them the next time you feel like making a spontaneous decision that promises to bring you joy instantly.

When you see images and examples portrayed by other people who seemingly have everything you want, it is natural to crave instant gratification at times. You want to get to where they are, and you want to get there fast. You don't usually see the hard work, effort, and struggles they had to get through—what you see is the end result. This can be deceiving because it might appear that they were able to receive instant gratification while striving for the same things you are. Naturally, this can be frustrating because you might feel that it is unfair that you have to go through all of these extra steps. The next time you witness someone who is successful, remind yourself that you are not seeing their whole journey. You are only seeing the end result. For all you know, they might still be facing struggles.

When you have a lot of uncertainty in your life, the options that promise instant gratification look attractive. You see a reward in front of you, so you believe that this is the best choice to strive for. As you will soon realise, instant gratification leaves you feeling empty after some time. When you understand how to reach for bigger goals, you will know that you are shorting yourself by choosing the instant gratification option. By aiming higher, you are making a permanent investment in your lasting happiness.

Chapter 7

Raise Your Words, Not Your Voice. Be an Adult

*It's not what happens to you,
but how you react to it that matters.*
—Epictetus

Your reactions to what happens to you say a lot more than your words ever can. Becoming emotionally mature has everything to do with the way you handle what life throws at you. It can mean the difference between you moving through life with grace and humility, versus you hitting the roof because something doesn't go your way. By knowing what to say and how to effectively use your voice to make a change, you will experience the greatest parts of life that are attainable and ready for you to take hold of.

*I used to think adulthood was
one crisis after another. I was wrong.
It is multiple crises in a row, consistently.*
(Self-Reference Jokes)

When you can make a commitment to improving your mindset, your life is going to get better. The things that once held you back, or debilitated you, will now only be small bumps along the road. You will have the right emotional tools necessary to face your problems and move forward in life. When you spend too much time focusing on what is wrong, it becomes easy to forget all that is right.

Avoiding Immaturity: Acknowledging the Signs

You might not be as mature as you think you are. While you go through the motions of adulthood, it is possible that you are still holding onto some emotionally immature behaviours. These can be corrected once they are recognised. Evaluate yourself and see if you can identify with any of these:

You Rely on Your Parents Too Much: It is great to have a close familial relationship, but still relying on your parents well into adulthood is a sign that you have yet to peak in emotional maturity. When you have your parents around to do everything for you, this gives you a way out of taking responsibility for your actions. It further enforces immature behaviour.

You Feel Out of Control: When something terrible happens to you, do you feel like you aren't going to recover from it? Immature people often cannot see that they have choices to make that can change their lives. If you simply let the bad things take over, those things are going to impact you in negative ways. Make sure you are using all of your resources whenever possible.

You Are Financially Dependent on Others: Getting financial help might be a necessity, but relying on other people to pay for your expenses all the time isn't healthy. If you aren't trying to gain financial independence, you are also not trying to progress in life. It isn't a realistic way to live, and it can create distance between you and others in your life who work hard for what they have.

You Have No Self-Control: If you feel the need to spend money impulsively or to cheat on your partner, this indicates that you have a problem with self-control. When you know something is wrong, yet you can't help but engage, this suggests that you are not acting from a mature mindset.

You Constantly Make Fun of Others: Talking down on other people makes you feel better about yourself when you have low self-esteem. For someone who isn't established, this can be an emotional outlet because there are few other ways that feel good when it comes to expressing yourself.

You Hate Being Alone: When you are alone with your own thoughts, are you uncomfortable? This can be a sign that something is going on that is impacting your mindset. If you are unhappy with your life in any way, these thoughts are surely going to rise to the surface when you have some quiet time. Distractions can only help the problem for so long.

You Don't Know How to Admit You Are Wrong: When you are wrong about something, you deny or ignore this rather than admitting that there was another solution—this definitely comes from a place of immaturity. It isn't easy to feel that you are wrong. Still, you can always learn from these moments instead of automatically reverting to shame.

You Blame Others for Your Mistakes: Instead of taking accountability for your actions, you would rather place the blame on other people. This feels good because it is almost like instant gratification. Your shame and guilt are instantly transferred, and you can continue on as nothing happened. This hurts people in the process.

Whether you can identify with one or all of these signs, there is a chance for you to make progress in life right now. You can work on these things by recognising that you do them. Once admitting that these are faults you rely on, you can then think of how to become more independent and accountable. We all need people to rely on at times, but no one should ever be made to fix all of your problems, not even your parents or your spouse. This is a lot of unfair pressure to put on another person. Remember, they are your loved ones, not your therapists.

Create healthy relationships with those in your life by talking openly about your struggles. You might be able to take away some valuable advice, but know that the hard work is up to you. It is you who must make an effort to change your patterns and to take control of your life. Even if you cannot predict what is going to happen, you can learn to be humble and to handle each situation with grace. Practice the art of acceptance. Once you do this, nothing will feel impossible.

Never feel like you are above an apology or an explanation. Each of these will help you become a more mature individual because they help you acknowledge what you are responsible for. There are going to be moments where you are not proud of your behaviour, but these moments are prime learning opportunities. You can take the lessons and turn them into habits that will prevent more mistakes from happening in the future. When you see failure as something that can help you rather than halt you, this is when you will grow as a person.

Growing from Failure

No matter how old you are, there is always room in your life to be a better adult. When you become set in your ways, nothing is going to change, but you already know this. To see real improvement, consider learning from your past failures. Try to find a lesson in each one that you can apply to your life right now. This is not only going to improve the situation, but it will also improve your happiness.

Pay Your Bills on Time

It goes without saying that paying your bills is important, but the way you handle your money says a lot about your maturity level. Suppose you are constantly behind on your payments or late with your bills because you are forgetful. In that case, you need to step it up—make it a priority to take care of these essential needs. Nothing else should take more importance than keeping a roof over your head, making sure you have electricity and being able to legally drive your car. Consider these things in relation to what else you'd like to spend money on. Shopping is nice, but living is necessary.

Always Try Your Best

It can be tempting to slack off when you do not have much pressure to do your best. To become more mature, you need to put this pressure on yourself. Do not make yourself feel debilitated, but make yourself feel like you should always try to your best. When you are not lazy or slacking off, you are going to feel great about the outcome of what you are doing. This instils a solid work ethic within, and it helps you when you do end up having to perform under pressure.

Treat Others with Respect

You do not need to agree with everyone around you; this is impossible. However, aim to respect everyone around you. No matter how different your opinions are, you can still treat others the way that you wish to be treated. This will say a lot about your maturity level. While it might be tempting to spite those with different views, that only makes you out to be a bully. Take the high road and rise above it.

Control Your Anger

It is okay to feel angry; this is going to happen to you. What matters is how you let it out. You do not need to lash out at other people to make yourself feel better. What you need is an outlet for your anger to filter through. You need to learn how to self-soothe and rationalise your thinking before your anger becomes too explosive. Get to the root of what is bothering you, find a way to release that negative energy, and make apologies whenever necessary. Blaming your anger on other people is not going to make you feel better inside.

Have a Life Plan

This can be a scary thought, especially if you haven't considered it in a while. Your life plan does not need to be a detailed map of what you are going to do in the next 20 years. You should, however, have an idea of some goals you'd like to achieve and how you plan on getting there. Having goals keeps you motivated; it gives your life a greater purpose. When you can focus on something productive, this gives you little room to get caught up on the small stuff.

Take Care of Yourself

If you feel that you are reaching a breaking point, stop pushing. You need to value both your physical and mental health. This is a big sign that you are mature. Everyone has different needs to feel good, and this extends beyond the basics of sleep and nourishment. You not only need to be functional, but you should also be happy. Take care of yourself in a way that nurtures the best parts of yourself. Give yourself what you need and do not wait around for other people to do this for you.

Don't Procrastinate

Most things *can* wait until later, but they shouldn't. Procrastination makes you lazy, and it puts you in a place where you might lose momentum with your productivity. When you procrastinate, your mind is becoming disengaged for some reason. You need to reel the focus back into what is important. Remind yourself of why you are doing the task, not just how you must do it. Having your goal in sight is going to keep you pushing forward.

Don't Leave People Hanging

When you cannot commit to other people, this is a sign of immaturity. This extends beyond romantic commitment. If you make plans with a friend, only to stop talking to them the day before you are going to confirm where you'd like to have lunch, this is flaky behaviour. You need to own up to your feelings. If you do not want to go for lunch, don't make plans. If the plans have already been discussed, respect your friend's time and give them the courtesy of a cancellation. The more you leave others hanging, the more you are sending a message that you only value yourself and your feelings.

Take up on these suggestions to improve yourself. It is never too late to realise that you want to become a better person, not only for the people around you but for yourself.

Becoming a Mature Adult

Don't wait for someone to call you out on your flaws—you can become mature right now with some effort. If you want to act like an adult and feel your independence, take some lessons from these tips.

- **Understand Cause and Effect**: Your actions are not inconsequential. Everything you say or do is going to cause some sort of reaction. Being mindful of this, think critically about the choices you make. Do not only consider yourself and your feelings.

- **Learn How to Work Hard**: Hard work gets you further in life; this is simple. If you are not willing to put in any hard work, you should not expect to be handed rewards and success. It takes effort to accomplish anything worthwhile.

- **Learn to Become Self-Reliant**: No matter how much support you have in your life, you must also learn how to be there for yourself. Understand what you need to do to take care of yourself, and make sure you can give yourself everything you need in life.

- **Practice Emotional Self-Regulation**: You must learn how to soothe yourself emotionally, without the input of other people. When you are experiencing an emotional crisis, you need to be sure you can calm yourself down and pick practical and safe coping mechanisms in the process. Your coping mechanisms are behaviours that allow you to remain happy and content. This includes writing down your feelings in a journal or taking some time to practice self-care.

- **Have Courage in Your Convictions**: When you firmly believe in something, stand by it. Even if you have yet to accomplish it yourself, you can still spread its message as something you believe in. This is a mature stance to take, especially when others might disagree with you. Life isn't always about getting everyone around you on the same page. It is about making the choices that are best for you and your life.

Emotional Maturity

Grasping the concept of emotional maturity can be difficult because you have learned habits since you were a child. These habits might be holding you back because you cannot see that there are better ways for you to function emotionally. If you want to get serious about improving your emotional maturity, you must be present in your life right now. Take a look at what is going on around you and how you are reacting to it. This table can help you differentiate emotionally mature actions versus emotionally immature actions.

Mature	Immature
Proactive	Reactive
Acting on emotions	Acting out emotions
Driven by purpose	Driven by habit
Holding onto love and abundance	Holding onto fear and scarcity
'Choose to' motivation	'Have to' motivation
Centred on giving	Centred on getting
Stepping beyond the comfort zone	Remaining locked into routines
Seeking growth	Avoiding failure
Living in the present	Living in the past or future
Having unity with others	Feeling separated from others

In life, you will experience key moments. These are events that can trigger emotional reactions. Making good choices when this happens isn't always easy. The stronger your emotions are, the more they have the power to sway you. The comparison table above should help you recognise what habits you can change to become more emotionally mature and less reactive when you experience a key moment.

It isn't through the calm moments of life that you have the opportunity to become more emotionally mature. This is why the key moments are essential. You learn during these times because they will often test you. When things seem to be going well, you are unlikely to take this time to make a change. Your key moments can become your catalysts for change. Use them wisely.

Always remain present, because this is going to give you the best chance of changing your current reality. If you are living for right now, you are going to be able to see everything come full circle. Teach yourself how to embrace reality. While a lot is happening in reality, there are some great moments to hold onto and cherish. Don't forget to do this, even if there is a lot of evil surrounding you. It is never too late to appreciate what you have and to express gratitude.

When you take any action, be responsible for this action. If you think critically about the choices you make, there should be little room to feel shame or guilt over what you are doing. Your actions often speak for you. No matter what you are doing, make sure that you will feel proud of them. Your actions are powerful, inspirational even. While you can use them to benefit yourself, you can also use them to help other people.

Practice integrity in everything you do. While there are ways to cheat the system so you end up on top, consider how that will make you feel—there is no sense of pride when you know you didn't work hard to get to where you are. Shortcuts are going to be available all around you. Many people you know might decide to take them, but this doesn't mean you have to go with the pack. If you keep up with your sense of integrity, this quality is going to shine through, and it is an admirable one.

Signs of Functionality

Now it is time to focus on the good that you do. These are some signs that you are a remarkable and functioning individual. Do not discount these behaviours because they are part of what makes you who you are. If you can identify with these habits, you should aim to find more like them. Take pride in the fact that you have been able to reach this point and that you have chosen to behave in this way. Functionality is a hard trait to accomplish, but you are on your way to becoming an even more functional version of yourself.

You Accept Feedback: You understand that feedback is not a direct attack on what you are doing; it can help you become even better. By graciously accepting feedback from other people, you know that these are merely opinions and offerings of advice— you do not need to take them to heart unless they speak to you. However, you can respect them still when they are given to you.

You Apologise Sincerely: An apology should never be forced or demanded. When you make a mistake, apologising from your heart is a wonderful trait to have. This shows how much you care about the person and the situation. You are showcasing your compassion and taking accountability for what you have said or done.

You Manage Your Time: You have a lot to do almost every day, yet you still manage your time effectively. Not only do you need to make sure you can complete your work, but you must also set aside some time for your partner, family, and loved ones. Don't forget about your alone time, either. Doing this is not easy, but having a great, time management plan helps to make your life more enjoyable.

You Understand When to Say "No": Saying no isn't easy, but it can be necessary. As you have learned, it is within your right to say no when something is not okay with you. This is a boundary you do not have to cross. When you say no to something detrimental, this shows that you value yourself. Whether it is about your time, energy, money, or something else, being able to say no is something you should feel very proud of.

You Can Empathise: When you practise empathy, you are directly relating to another person and what they are going through. This shows that you can step outside of yourself and your problems to focus on someone else or something else. It is a great experience because a lot of people need compassion to feel loved. You can spread so much love by simply acting in an empathetic way.

You Make Friends with Different People: Broadening your friendship horizon isn't the easiest. Still, when you can effectively communicate with others, you are bound to make more friends. Being able to befriend those in different groups, communities, and situations will create more diversity around you. This is important because it can teach you how you are privileged in some ways and how you should aspire to be in other ways.

You Know How to Budget: Creating a budget for yourself doesn't mean that you cannot spend any money. What it means is that you know how much money is coming in, how much money you owe in debt, and how much you have left over. With this extra money, you can decide if you'd like to save it, spend it, or both. Having a personal budget is a brilliant and mature decision for anyone to make.

You Spend Time Alone: When you are constantly around other people, this gives you very little time to check in with yourself. Just as you would with a friend, have some time to yourself to see how you are doing. This is going to keep you in touch with your emotions in a healthy way.

Everyone can benefit from some occasional alone time. Not only is it informative, but it is also very relaxing.

You Ask for Help: Being functional does not mean you know everything there is to know; it means that you use your resources. If you need help, do not be ashamed to ask for it. There are many people out there who have valuable knowledge that they are willing to share with you. Think about this as an additional way to expand your knowledge and your skills.

If you can recognise these traits in yourself, feel proud of the great qualities you possess. These signs of functionality are all positive habits to maintain, and they make your life feel more abundant and efficient. For the traits you do not see in yourself, there is time to learn them. Understand that building habits can take time, but it is a worthwhile effort to make.

Chapter 8

Forgiving Yourself. Forgiving Others

Start by doing what's necessary, then do what's possible; and suddenly you are doing the impossible.
—Francis of Assisi

No matter what, you must find forgiveness in your heart. This does not only apply to other people who do you wrong—being able to forgive yourself is a big part of your healing journey. The idea behind forgiveness is that it is enriching and therapeutic. It also comes from a place deep within your spirituality. You must understand what is wrong and how to move past it in order to forgive. This process symbolises a lot of growth within, allowing you to feel better capable when handling difficult situations.

When you forgive yourself for what you have been through in the past, you are giving yourself the peace of mind to live better in the present. You are also giving yourself a chance to showcase all of your strengths. Forgiveness is not weakness; it is the exact opposite. To forgive yourself, you must come from a deep place of self-awareness.

This needs to be addressed before you can move on. It is a big step to take, especially during times when you feel you were wronged.

Everyone in life has limitations, yourself included. Just because some move on from hard times faster than others, does not mean there is anything wrong with you if you need extra time. Respect your limits and boundaries, just as you would with anyone else you care about. Your limitations do not make you a failure; they are merely traits that you must work with. Once you forgive yourself, you will see that there are some imperfections in your actions—this is normal. Nobody gets everything right on the first try.

Once you forgive yourself for all you have been holding onto, you will have much more room in your present for new experiences. The memories of the past won't be able to hold you back or prevent you from doing something similar again. It is like riding a horse—you must get back on, even if you fall off. Your mistakes are not going to ruin your life. They will push you to your limits, make you uncomfortable, but they will not break you. Tell yourself this until you truly believe it. Understand that learning is a positive experience, and through self-forgiveness, there is plenty of growth. You will understand how to be more compassionate and more rational. The mistakes you made once before won't always come back again in the same way in your future.

Release any anger or hard feelings you still have about the situation. No matter how long ago it occurred, you have every right to feel something about it. Find an outlet where you can express these things. Whether you need to journal about it every day or seek therapy to get to the bottom of things, this first stage is about the release. Next, remind yourself that you deserve to be free of this pain and emotional discomfort. You do not need to live your life carrying any burdens once you have already learned each lesson from them.

This is how the process of healing begins. You might have to remind yourself to keep your heart open to forgiveness and to forgive yourself for realising that you are worthy of happiness. You do not need to suffer because of something that happened in your past. Accept it, learn from it, and move on from it. Some days, this will feel easier to do, but even on the hard days, remind yourself that there is so much more of your life you have yet to live. Think about all of the experiences that you will have that will go right.

The Four Rs of Self-Forgiveness

For a quick way to ensure you are self-forgiving, you can follow these simple steps. These are known as the four Rs of self-forgiveness, and they should make the process easier for you.

Responsibility: Accept what has happened, no matter what this is. You cannot put the past behind you when you want to forgive yourself. Acknowledge the role you played, and then show yourself some compassion.

Remorse: Once you complete the first step, you will likely be met with many emotions—sometimes shame and guilt. These negative emotions are natural to feel, but you must understand that any mistakes you have made do not signify that you are a bad person.

Restoration: You must make amends with those you have hurt, yourself included. This is a massive part of the self-forgiveness process. Provide apologies if they are necessary, and aim to restore the trust that existed before the event occurred. While the level of trust that existed before might feel different now, the actions and words are still sincere. This will show the other person that you truly value having them in your life.

Renewal: This final step urges you to move forward. Everyone makes mistakes, but falling into a self-hatred trap is not going to do you any good. It also will not erase the mistakes of the past. Find a way to learn from the experience; this will help you grow as a person.

To further enhance your ability to forgive yourself, make sure that you keep the four Rs in mind. They will guide you towards more accepting habits.

Forgiveness Can Be a Challenge

Forgiving yourself is quite the task, but forgiving others can be even more difficult. This is mostly true when they have hurt or betrayed you very badly. Holding onto that negativity for the rest of your life isn't healthy at all. Even if this person is no longer in your life and you never speak to them again, you can find forgiveness for them in your heart. This is not for their benefit, but your own. You deserve to have peace and tranquillity. Your past did shape you in many ways, but it is not who you are as a person.

When you want to forgive someone, your anger can clearly get in the way. Anger is another form of passion, and it can cloud your judgement. Even if the person apologises to you first and reforms their behaviour, your anger is only going to show you the hurtful actions they have taken against you. It is hard to just move on from things this way. When enough anger is present, this takes away your self-control. This is why it feels nearly impossible to have a casual conversation with someone who has just wronged you. Your anger triggers your fight-or-flight response, and it is telling you to fight.

The way that you speak about the incident also makes a big difference. If you remember something as traumatic and awful, hearing the other person describe it as anything less can feel very triggering. Since you each have your own perspective of the matter, there are going to be some discrepancies in the way you individually feel. Know that you do not have to convince them to feel the way you do; you should not fight to change their mind. Instead, stand firmly behind your own feelings and bring up points that support why you feel this way. This is going to be much more empowering than challenging the other person.

Fear is another reason why forgiveness can be so painful. You've been hurt, so you do not want to get hurt again. This is human nature, and you should never feel ashamed if you feel this way. Nobody sets out to seek other people or situations that will hurt them; this isn't a healthy way to live. In some ways, forgiveness can almost feel like you are giving the person permission to harm you or violate you again in the same way. In fear of being disappointed, you prolong the process of forgiveness and end up never dealing with the consequences of holding that kind of negativity inside you.

When something terrible happens to you, a part of you might believe the other person isn't worthy of forgiveness. Instead, you wish that they could be punished for what they have done. In some cases, you do get this kind of gratification. Any situation involving the law gives you this kind of a justice opportunity, but most general disputes will not. Since you do not get to choose this, it can feel very frustrating. All of the bad energy you spend putting towards them should instead be focused inward on your healing. Build yourself up, even if you know that they are a horrible person. Do not give them any more of your time and attention than they have already taken.

Misunderstandings shake things up when it comes to forgiveness. When you have a misunderstanding with someone, this can feel embarrassing. You might immediately realise you are in the wrong or come to this conclusion at some point. Instead of ignoring the discovery, you need to be the bigger person—forgive them for what happened, especially when you realise it wasn't entirely their fault. Own up to your own behaviour and explain why you reacted the way you did. This kind of clarity can save friendships and relationships. It shows that you do not see yourself in higher regard than anyone else, a humble approach to take. Having this quality makes you a likeable and a more approachable person. Things do not always have to result in a conflict or argument to be resolved.

Myths About Forgiveness

As you are working through the process of forgiveness, you must remember what it does not include. Many myths surround forgiveness that leads people to believe it is difficult or time-consuming. It doesn't have to be! The process is as simple as you make it. With the right techniques, you will be able to forgive yourself and those who have hurt you. Show yourself that you have this kind of strength, and ignore the myths that often hold you back.

When You Forgive, You Forget

You might remember some situations for the rest of your life; forgiveness does not erase them. Forgiveness is simply supposed to give you peace of mind and the ability to move on. If memories of your past come up, allow them to enter your brain before watching them leave. By acknowledging them without holding onto them, you can find a healthy balance between forgiveness and letting go. You should never aim to forget what happened because this will likely lead to repressed memories. This is detrimental because it means you are still holding onto the pain and negativity of the past.

You Are Ignoring the Other's Actions

By forgiving someone, you are not ignoring or excusing what they have done. That is on their conscience and for them to deal with. Forgiveness must be done for *you* to heal. Do not worry about how the other person will get through it, because they need to figure that out on their own. You are not ignoring their actions, but simply forcing them to take responsibility for them. When they are left alone with their thoughts, knowing that you are at peace, any guilt they have is going to weigh heavily on them.

Forgiveness Will Fix Your Relationship with the Other Person

Just because you both agree to forgive one another does not mean you will automatically be able to continue your friendship/relationship/connection. A betrayal changes the dynamic in some ways, often preventing things from feeling the same as they used to. You must either work together to mend the bond you had, or you can choose to separate from one another if the dynamic is toxic. An apology can fix a lot of emotional turmoil, but it will not necessarily mend any of your relationships.

You Need to *Feel* Forgiving

This is untrue. You might be extremely annoyed with the other person, even after time has gone by, but you can still find it within yourself to forgive them. This is about you moving on, letting go of the negativity and anger that still plagues you. If you have strong feelings about a situation still, this is an indication that you are not as 'over it' as you think you are. Separate the notion that forgiveness must be done gently and kindly. Things might get complicated and messy, but that is life. Nothing is perfect, and you don't have to pretend that it is.

You Only Need to Forgive Once

In some cases, a situation might call for several apologies. Life is very complex in this way. When something happens, and you talk about it, several issues have the chance to arise. What you might believe fixes one problem, only opens the door to more. Be patient and forgive wisely, even if the other person has a lot to be sorry for. Part of growing as an individual is getting better at communicating with others. If something still isn't sitting right with you about the situation, let them know.

Forgiveness Restores the Original Balance

Forgiveness is a powerful weapon, but it does not mean that the dynamic is going to go back to the way it was. People get hurt, and things change. You might not be as close to someone who hurt you as you once were, but this does not mean you need to give up on your connection. The dynamic is likely to change, and you need to either earn one another's trust back or figure out how to move on in the most amicable way you can. Do not hold out hope for an apology that turns back time; this isn't possible. No matter how much you wish things could be the same, they are different now; you must learn how to grow.

Means Towards Forgiveness

On the path to forgiveness, the entire process becomes simpler when you take it in steps. You cannot expect yourself to forgive someone who hurt you overnight, but you can work on getting there by working on this process. These are the blueprints that you will use to take you towards the path of forgiveness.

By taking these steps, you are going to make the process of forgiveness easier on yourself. Remember that nobody is perfect, and keep this in mind as you work on the type of forgiveness that you require to move on.

1. **Express Yourself**: If you sugarcoat anything, you will not be taking a realistic look at the problem. When you have a goal of forgiveness in mind, you must express yourself. Sometimes, these feelings and thoughts aren't going to be the most positive but now is your chance to get them out. Stop holding onto them and letting them torment you.

    If you would like to maintain this connection to the person you are trying to forgive, only speak from your own perspective. Tell them exactly how the situation made you feel and how you feel about it now. Try to get them to understand your perspective and where you are coming from. No matter how well you know each other, you should never assume that they can read your mind and fully understand your feelings. You need to vocalise them.

2. **Look for the Positive**: Before you try to approach the person you'd like to forgive, journal about what happened. Try to pull every single detail you can remember, and consider things from your perspective. After you have written it all down, focus on any positive outlooks you can find. Are you stronger now because of it? Did it teach you how to value yourself more? You need to play to the strengths that you have obtained.

When you are ready to talk to this person, you will also be coming from a much more positive approach. Being prepared to put the situation behind you is necessary. If you come with confrontation, the problem will likely get worse. You might then end up having to forgive them for two separate instances. Almost every negative situation has a silver lining; you must look for it. Use it to guide you.

3. **Create Empathy**: When you are speaking to someone, they are highly likely to mirror the energy you present to them. Coming from a place of empathy puts a calming aspect on almost any situation. When you act empathetic, you are showing the other person that you want to understand, not argue. Even if you do not agree with one another, you can still find ways to better understand where you are coming from. You might have to agree to disagree, but this is better than feuding for years at a time.

   You do not need to see this person as your 'enemy'. This will only cultivate negative energy, blocking you from feeling any empathy. You can see them as someone who has a different viewpoint than your own. While it might infuriate you or confuse you, do your best to keep an open mind. Remain firm to your own beliefs and morals though. Mature people are able to converse about things they disagree with while also being able to forgive one another for past outbursts.

4. **Protect Yourself**: Even if the incident happened long ago, you still need to protect yourself from being hurt any further by it. As you are discussing the issue, remind yourself that you are already far removed from it. While it still impacts

you emotionally, you do not need to let it take over your life. It happened, and it is done. The only focus should be on resolving it now. If the other person starts to become too combative, take back your control. Step away for a breather or speak up; you do not have to tolerate it.

If you can tell that this person does not have a goal of resolution like you do, it is okay to call it a loss. As long as you have said what you wanted to say, then you can free your mind of this situation that used to bother you. Human connections are complicated, and feelings can complicate things even further. Allow yourself to walk away from people and situations that are toxic because they are only going to continue hurting you if there is no point of resolution.

5. **Get Help**: Even if you forgive the other person for what has happened, it is normal to have lingering feelings and emotions. Therapy can be very helpful for getting the rest of your feelings out. By working with a professional, you can come up with some strategies together that will help you cope when things feel manageable. There is no problem too big or too small that wouldn't benefit from therapy. Do some research and see if you can sign up for a consultation with a therapist in

your area. Nowadays, there are also online therapy options for those who do not feel comfortable going in person; both are valid.

If you can talk to a friend or someone you trust about the problems you face, do this! Venting your frustrations alleviates tension. It is healthy and harmless, especially when you have a listening ear who is very willing to hear what you have to say. It is okay to rely on your support system because that is what they are there for. They want to help you too.

Being Kind to Yourself

Being kind to yourself is like the aftercare of forgiveness. You have just gone through a lot of emotional stress, so it makes sense to be very kind to yourself to boost your morale. When you are more kind to yourself, you are building up your trust in yourself. This will help you in many aspects, especially with your self-confidence that might have been shattered by people or situations in your past. We tend to be our own worst critics, coming down harshly on ourselves with judgements we would never impose on other people. You need to make sure you care about yourself as much as you care about your loved ones. Treat yourself the way you'd treat your best friend.

In the process of being kind to yourself, you must also push yourself to do better and be a better person. This is going to prevent you from feeling any regret or doubt that you aren't doing the best you can. Being kind is hard enough, but putting in the hard work to seal the deal presents its own challenges. You must work through them with grace, accepting that this is part of the healing process. This is what will make you a strong person that people will look up to for inspiration.

When you feel the need to be harsh on yourself for making a mistake or not doing something as planned, think about what you can do right now to remedy the situation. Instead of being down on yourself because you forgot to water your plants for three days, what else can you do? Water them now. The time that you would spend being hard on yourself, potentially blaming yourself for not taking great care of them can be spent in a much more positive way. Most situations that encompass blame can be handled in this way. You need to act proactively, always considering what you can do instead of what you cannot do. If it is in the past, there is honestly no reason to speculate on what you could have done.

Instead of focusing on your flaws, devote your time to making yourself better and praising yourself for the great qualities you have. This kind of balance can restore your self-confidence. Nothing in life is all bad or all good;

there is a mixture of both in almost any person and situation. Learn how to bring more of the good to the surface. Appreciate the things you do that keep your life running smoothly and make others happy. They are being noticed more than you realise, and other people appreciate you for who you are.

Always remind yourself that you have a kind heart. The heart works from within, dictating how your body is cared for and how you treat other people. It is a very powerful muscle. If you know in your heart that you are capable of kindness, you are already off to a fantastic start. Nobody is born inherently evil or terrible at making decisions. These traits are learned, and habits enforced them.

When you notice your flaws, accept them. Maybe you want to lose a little weight. This is an opinion, but it does not prevent you from being a wonderful partner, a great friend, and an excellent employee. This is simply an aspect of yourself that you would like to work on, not a hindrance. Having personal goals is great when you can be kind to how you approach them. Tell yourself that you might have flaws, but you also have many redeeming qualities. List them. Remind yourself what they are regularly to further promote balance in your life. You have the ability to heal yourself and make the most of your current situation. Through this process, you will realise how strong and amazing you truly are.

Conclusion

Healing yourself can often become a lifelong process, but one that fills you with wisdom and courage. No matter what you have been through, what you are going through, or what you will go through, believe in yourself and your strength. Through the skills you uncovered about yourself as you read this book, you should feel inspired and empowered to live your life to the fullest. Mistakes are often made, and unpredictable events will happen to you, but this does not mean you need to stop your life in your tracks. You have what it takes to heal yourself and get through this.

It all starts when you focus on your core beliefs. These are the principles you live by that should never be broken. Living for a purpose, you will have a better idea of when you need to stand your ground. In doing so, this makes you more mindful and observant. By understanding the world around you and how other people think, you will not feel so caught up in your own ways and routines. There are many different avenues to the same location.

The road to recovery is a journey, sometimes a long one. Be patient with yourself as you figure it out. During this process, you should work on bettering yourself, becoming more emotionally mature, and connecting to the process of healing. In the end, you are going to come out of this feeling strong and refreshed. The wounds of your past will no longer have a hold over you. Forgiveness is key. If you cannot forgive yourself and the other person involved, you will continue to suffer from the situation.

When you are willing to put in the work, you will feel like a well-rounded individual who can carefully assess different situations and different emotional connections. With your hard work involved, you will feel very accomplished after realising that this is all it takes to commit to your healing process. Putting in the effort towards something important is never pointless or nonsensical. Your feelings are always valid, and you need to listen to them if you'd like them to guide you along the way.

Now, you have all the tools you need to change your life for the better. You can finally heal from your past wounds and prepare yourself for any challenges you encounter in the future. If you enjoyed reading this book and learning more about the healing process and your emotions, do not hesitate to leave a review on Amazon that explains your journey so far. This book is supposed to help you in the long run, not only for the moment. Be confident and believe in your ability to do this—anything is possible.

References

5 Facts About Self-Awareness | Psychologia. (n.d.). Psychologia https://psychologia.co/5-facts-about-self-awareness/

A Conscious Rethink. (2020, July 15). *How To Grow Up And Be A Mature Adult: 13 No Bullsh*t Lessons!* A Conscious Rethink. https://www.aconsciousrethink.com/10841/how-to-grow-up-mature-adult/

Allen, R. (2020, April 18). *How to Become Emotionally Mature: Roger K. Allen.* Roger K Allen, Conflict Management, Listening Skills, Self Empowerment. https://www.rogerkallen.com/how-to-become-emotionally-mature/

Babauta, L. *How to be Kind to Yourself & Still Get Stuff Done.* Zen Habits. https://zenhabits.net/kind-done/

Beard, C. (2019, December 27). *Everything You Need To Know About Mindfulness.* The Blissful Mind https://theblissfulmind.com/mindfulness-basics/

Brandon, J. (2019, September 16). *Science Says There's a Simple Reason You Keep Thinking Negative Thoughts*

All Day. Inc. https://www.inc.com/john-brandon/science-says-theres-a-simple-reason-you-keep-thinking-negative-thoughts-all-day.html

Burton, N. (2014, May 7). *The Very Best Psychology Jokes*. Psychology Today. https://www.psychologytoday.com/us/blog/hide-and-seek/2001405/the-very-best-psychology-jokes.

Cherry, K. (2020, June 29). *How to Forgive Yourself*. Very Well Mind. https://www.verywellmind.com/how-to-forgive-yourself-4583819.

Clarke, S. (2019, March 18). *Examples Of Core Beliefs And How To Change Yours*. Down to Earth Mental Health Talk https://projectenergise.com/examples-of-core-beliefs/

Fox, D. (2018, November 3). *Why it's Totally Okay to Change Your Life Path (and Why You Should!)*. Wonder Forest. https://www.thewonderforest.com/2016/06/totally-okay-change-life-path.html.

Gelles, D. (n.d.). *How to Be More Mindful at Work*. The New York Times https://www.nytimes.com/guides/well/be-more-mindful-at-work

Hansen, R. (2013, December 13). *The 10-Step Plan to Changing Your Career*. LiveCareer. https://

www.livecareer.com/resources/careers/planning/career-change.

Hill, T. (2015, July 16). *Attachment Re-visited: 7 Red Flag Signs of Poor Boundaries.* PsychCentral https://blogs.psychcentral.com/caregivers/2015/07/emotional-attachment-10-red-flag-signs-of-poor-boundaries/

How to become self-aware. (n.d.). ReachOut.com https://au.reachout.com/articles/how-to-become-self-aware

Imafidon, C. (2015, October 4). *This Is Why You Should Forgive Yourself, No Matter What.* Lifehack https://www.lifehack.org/316764/this-why-you-should-forgive-yourself-matter-what-2.

Ishak, R. (2016, October 18). *9 Signs You're Probably Not As Mature As You Think You Are & How To Fix The Problem.* Bustle. https://www.bustle.com/articles/171525-9-signs-youre-probably-not-as-mature-as-you-think-you-are-how-to-fix.

Lebowitz, S. (2019, April 2). *19 signs you're a functioning adult - even if it doesn't feel like it.* Business Insider. https://www.businessinsider.com/signs-of-adulthood-2016-8?r=US.

Lee, K. (2018, September 11). *Why Is It So Hard to Set Boundaries?* Psychology Today https://www.psychologytoday.com/us/blog/rethink-your-way-the-good-life/201809/why-is-it-so-hard-set-boundaries

Limericks about Love. (2019, October 19). Limericks About Love https://kingoflimericks.com/limericks-about-love/

Live Science Staff. (2016, March 25). *Understanding the 10 Most Destructive Human Behaviours.* LiveScience. https://www.livescience.com/14152-destructive-human-behaviours-bad-habits.html.

Manson, M. (2020, July 16). *Why You Suck at Self-Awareness.* Mark Manson https://markmanson.net/self-awareness

Martin, S. (2020, January 26). *What Are Boundaries and Why Do I Need Them?* Sharon Martin https://livewellwithsharonmartin.com/what-are-boundaries/

McAllister, D. (2019, March 1). *6 Myths About Forgiveness.* TheHopeLine. https://www.thehopeline.com/what-forgiveness-is-not-part-2/.

McArthur Aged Care. *Understanding Professional Boundaries.* McArthur Aged Care.

Morgan, C. (2017, June 13). *How to Be an Adult: 15 Mature Ways to Grow Up and Behave Like One.* LovePanky.

https://www.lovepanky.com/my-life/better-life/how-to-be-an-adult.

Morin, A. (2017, September 04). *3 Important Ways Your Childhood Shaped Who You Are.* Psychology Today https://www.psychologytoday.com/us/blog/what-mentally-strong-people-dont-do/201709/3-important-ways-your-childhood-shaped-who-you-are

Nelson, M. (2018, January 25). *5 Reasons Why It's Hard to Forgive People.* Psych2Go. https://psych2go.net/5-reasons-hard-forgive-people/

O'Brien, M. (2019, April 23). *11 Ways to Bring More Mindfulness Into Your Daily Life Today.* Melli O'Brien https://mrsmindfulness.com/11-ways-to-bring-more-mindfulness-into-your-life-today/

Podcast. Mindfulness, meaning & purpose, moment by moment. Active Pause https://activepause.com/proactive-reactive/

Scott, E. (2020, March 3). *5 Effective Strategies to Forgive Others and Move On.* Verywell Mind. https://www.verywellmind.com/how-to-forgive-3144957

Self-awareness is the first step to personality development. (n.d.). Spiritual Science Research Foundation https://www.spiritualresearchfoundation.org/

spiritual-practice/steps-of-spiritual-practice/
personality-defect-removal-and-improvement/
self-awareness/?gclid=CjwKCAjw_-D3BRBIEiwA-
jVMy7Mzya4dFdcLsjFurV_lh9CAbVicZCrj-ESz5MpC-
JF1rRm7IRZqOivRoCKPoQAvD_BwE

SELF-REFERENCE JOKES. (n.d.). Self-Reference Jokes: A Collection https://web.maths.unsw.edu.au/~jim/selfref.html

Setting Boundaries in a Relationship. Break the Cycle. (2017, February 15). https://www.breakthecycle.org/blog/setting-boundaries-relationship.

Shankar, S. (2016, September 25). *7 ways to clear your mind of negative thoughts. Wisdom* by Gurudev Sri Sri Ravi Shankar https://wisdom.srisriravishankar.org/clear-your-mind-of-negative-thoughts/?keyword=

Star, K. (2020, April 10). *How Thoughts and Values May Affect Your Anxiety.* Very Well Mind https://www.verywellmind.com/negative-thinking-patterns-and-beliefs-2584084

Tash of The Reflective Mind. (2020, June 02). *6 Unique Ways To Be Mindful Of Others.* The Reflective Mind https://the-reflective-mind.com/mindfulness-of-others/

Tartakovsky, M. (2018, July 08). *6 Subtle Signs Your Boundaries Are Being Broken.* PsychCentral https://psychcentral.com/blog/6-subtle-signs-your-boundaries-are-being-broken/

Three Social Awareness Skills You Need In A Relationship Dr Georgiana. (n.d.). Dr Georgiana http://www.drgeorgiana.com/social-awareness-skills-you-need-in-a-relationship/

Tobak, S. (2013, March 29). *7 Signs You're Not Self-Aware Enough to Be a Great Leader.* Inc. https://www.inc.com/steve-tobak/7-signs-youre-not-as-self-aware-as-you-think.html

Weiss, S. (2019, March 31). *How To Set Boundaries With Your Family, According To A Life Coach.* Bustle https://www.bustle.com/p/how-to-set-boundaries-with-your-family-according-to-a-life-coach-16980926

Well, T. (2019, September 30). *Can You Be Too Self-Aware?* Psychology Today https://www.psychologytoday.com/gb/blog/the-clarity/201909/can-you-be-too-self-aware

Westacott, E. (2020, February 26). *Do You Know The Meaning of The Good Life?* ThoughtCo. https://www.thoughtco.com/what-is-the-good-life-4038226

Williams, A. (2015, July 09). *Core Beliefs Part 1: Identifying and Understanding Core Beliefs*. Rowan Center for Behavioural Medicine https://www.rowancenterla.com/new-blog/2015/7/9/core-beliefs-part-1-identifying-and-understanding-core-beliefs

Zadro, S. (2019, April 09). *How to shift the negative core beliefs that stem from childhood*. WellBeing https://www.wellbeing.com.au/mind-spirit/mind/core-beliefs-negative-mind.html

Printed in Great Britain
by Amazon